Dr H J Witteveen was born in 1921 in Zeist, The Netherlands, and grew up in a Sufi family. From an early age he was inspired by the wisdom of Sufism. Initiated at the age of 18, he has made a life-long study of the Sufi message combining his inner life with his business activities. He is currently Vice-President of the International Sufi Movement and an economic advisor.

Universal Sufism

H. J. WITTEVEEN

ELEMENT
Shaftesbury, Dorset • Rockport, Massachusetts
Melbourne, Victoria

For Ratan, my dear companion on life's path.

First published in Great Britain in 1997 by
Element Books Limited
Shaftesbury, Dorset SP7 8BP

Published in the USA in 1997 by
Element Books, Inc.
PO Box 830, Rockport, MA 01966

2/98

Published in Australia in 1997 by
Element Books Limited
and distributed by Penguin Australia Ltd
487 Maroondah Highway, Ringwood, Victoria 3134

Design by Roger Lightfoot
Cover design by Max Fairbrother
Typeset by Westkey Limited, Falmouth, Cornwall
Printed and bound in Great Britain by
Creative Print and Design (Wales), Ebbw Vale

British Library Cataloguing in Publication Data available

Library of Congress Cataloging in Publication Data available

ISBN 1-86204-093-1

Contents

List of Figures

List of Plate Illustrations

Black and White Plates

Colour Plates

Picture Credits

The author and publishers would like to thank the following for permission to use illustrations:

The Bookworks, California for the figure 'Pattern of sound waves, caused by moving along a steel plate' from *Seeing with the Mind's Eye* by Mike and Nancy Samuels (Random House, London, 1988);

Dover Publications Inc for the figures 'The radiation spectrum', 'Orbit of an electron', 'Vibration analogy', 'The soul, mind and the body' from *Music of the Spheres* by Guy Murchie (New York, 1967);

East-West Publications and Sufi Foundation Inayat for 'Hazrat Inayat Khan with a group of *mureeds*', 'An interview with Hazrat Inayat Khan' and 'Inayat Khan braving the storm' by Saida van Tuyll van Serooskerken in *The Flower Garden* (London/The Hague, 1978);

the International Headquarters of the Sufi Movement for the portrait of Maulabaskhsh, the photograph of Inayat Khan's birthplace, the photograph of Inayat Khan's mother, the photographs of Inayat Khan as a young man and in later life, the copy of the article from *Southern Daily Echo*, 9 April 1919, and the photograph of Inayat Khan in the garden at Suresnes;

Bert van Liempd for his photographs of the *dargah* of Nizam-ud-Din Aulia, the courtyard in front of Inayat Khan's *dargah* in New Delhi, Inayat Khan's *dargah* and the Sufi temple Universal Murad Hassil at Katwijk;

the National Museum of New Delhi for the cover illustration of 'A Sufi Teacher (Murshid) and his Disciples (*mureeds*)' and the picture 'Sufi Discipleship'.

Every effort has been made to trace all copyright holders, but if any have been inadvertently overlooked the author and publishers will be pleased to make the necessary arrangement at the first opportunity.

Preface

This book is a reflection of the immense blessing and inspiration that the Sufi message of Hazrat Inayat Khan has been in my life. I have continued to study it but not in an academic way, for Sufism needs to be lived. The Sufi ideal is to maintain balance between the inner and outer life. I have tried to follow that ideal during my active life as an economist.

When one has found something of great value one naturally wishes to share it. That is why I have written this book which introduces the rich world of universal Sufism. In explaining different aspects of the Sufi message I have often quoted Hazrat Inayat Khan's own words as these can best convey his mystical inspiration.

In presenting this book I would like also to express my thankfulness to the many Sufis who have inspired me over the years, helping me to understand and to realize the great richness and depths of the Sufi message.

First I should mention my parents. I owe it to them that I grew up in a Sufi atmosphere and that the Sufi teachings were brought to me with great clarity and simplicity when I still was a boy. I also must thank my first initiator, Kafia Blaauw-Robertson, who gave me my first Sufi practices in a very inspiring manner. Later I was privileged to receive spiritual guidance from the great mystics and companions of Hazrat Inayat Khan, Muhammad Ali Khan and Musharaff Khan, and later from Inayat Khan's grandson Fazal Inayat Khan. I became involved in the leadership of the Sufi movement and this brought me into close contact with these remarkable personalities. Through my whole adult life I have studied Inayat Khan's teachings and participated in different activities of the Sufi movement. I now continue the Sufi work in harmonious cooperation with the present leader of the Sufi movement, Hidayat Inayat Khan, the second son of Hazrat Inayat Khan. There have been many stimulating discussions and a deep friendship with many other Sufi *mureeds* (disciples in the inner school of Sufism). I am especially grateful to Ratan, my wife, who has always supported and inspired me in this work while we pursued the Sufi path together.

In my work on this book I have been stimulated by many suggestions from Leonard Appel, the brilliant editor of the magazine *Initiations* in Brussels, who first brought up the idea of such a book. Shaikh-ul-mashaikh Mahmood Khan, a cousin of Inayat Khan, who has studied classical Sufism extensively, made an important contribution to the first chapter on the history of Sufism. I am greatly indebted to him. Of course the way in which I have used his contributions remains my own responsibility.

Then my thanks go to my successive secretaries: Ms Ria Sampimon, Ms Patricia Meuws and Ms Dorien de Jonge, who made their essential contributions by accurately typing parts of the manuscript. Finally I very much appreciated the contribution of Jess Curtis, my English editor, who made many thoughtful improvements in the English text of my book.

Nevertheless, I remain conscious of the fact that an attempt to describe the Sufi message will always remain inadequate. Sufism is much more than what can be put into words and ideas, for it is not a theory, it has no dogma. It is a way of life, an attitude. It is characterized by a certain atmosphere of peace, of a deeper reality. I hope that something of that atmosphere will shine through the veil of my written explanations.

Introduction

On 13 September 1910 the great Indian mystic and musician Hazrat Inayat Khan departed from Bombay by boat for the United States of America. He was accompanied by his brother, Maheboob Khan, and his cousin Muhammad Ali Khan. His aim was to bring a message of Sufism, of inner wisdom, to the world, harmonizing East and West. He undertook this difficult task with deep faith in his divine mission.

The world of America that he discovered was totally strange to him, in many ways quite opposite to the Indian world of that time. He observed it, listened to it and was inspired to give his Sufi message as an answer to the questions of that Western world. In doing this he modernized the age-old Sufi wisdom and made it universal, so that it could emerge from the Islamic context in which it had developed for centuries.

The Universal Sufism that he brought to the world thus offers a deeply satisfying answer to the need of the present time. For in an integrating world, where all cultures and religions come into closer contact, there is clearly a great need for understanding and harmony between the religions. For this purpose Inayat Khan created the Universal Worship, which brings all religions together in one inspiring religious service (see chapter 7). He shows that there is an essential unity between the great religions of the world. He sees a divine inspiration which comes to humanity from time to time in differing forms which are in harmony with the culture of a certain people at a certain time. Different forms but the same essential truth.

And in our scientific and specializing world, where relig- ious traditions and dogmas often conflict with a scientific world view, Universal Sufism offers a mystical philosophy, in line with the findings of modern science on the one hand and with mysticism and religion on the other. Here Inayat Khan's great contribution to Sufism is his fusion of renewed classical Sufism, personal creative originality and universal focus. A comprehensive and universal vision such as this is greatly needed in the present state of human consciousness (chapter 5).

What is needed above all is a way for modern man to re-establish contact with his inner being through meditation. The Sufi Order, the esoteric school of inner culture of the Sufi movement, gives serious seekers access to a way of spiritual guidance and training which has proved its value over centuries. Here Inayat Khan maintains the terms and tech- niques of classical Sufism. In order to arrive at the realization of the one universal truth one has to follow one particular path of practices; there is no mixing of different techniques. Inspired by his personal experience Inayat Khan renewed these esoteric exercises. Thus this mystical tradition, that has lived continuously since the 7th Century, has now received a new life-impulse from this great present-time spiritual teacher and mystic. And this approach to meditation and the inner life does not require a turning away from the outer life; on the contrary it inspires and strengthens us to do our work and fulfil our obligations. Life in the world is considered positively, as an opportunity to learn and to widen our consciousness, preparing us in this way for mystical experi- ence. Balance between inner and outer life is the Sufi ideal (chapter 8).

To show something of the different ways in which this mystical wisdom has been expressed over time, the first chapter gives an overview of the progress of Sufism through the centuries. Starting with the origins of mysticism in the ancient Egyptian mysteries, it then describes some mystical moments of great Sufis in the Islamic Middle East, finally moving to the Indian Chishtia order into which Inayat Khan was initiated. In chapter 2 the focus is on Inayat Khan: the world in which he grew up, his musical career and his extraordinary spiritual search which prepared him for his great task in the West. Some highlights of his life and work in the West follow. To give something of the flavour and atmosphere of the Sufi message, a few personal reminiscences of Inayat Khan's first disciples have been included. In the following chapters different aspects of Sufi teachings are described, often using Inayat Khan's own words – but also illustrating how these ideas converge with other lines of present-day thinking.

The final chapter holds out the idea of peace. This is what the world now needs more than anything else. But the possibility of building a harmonious and peaceful world depends on the spiritual evolution of mankind, for it is only through this evolution that man can widen his consciousness and overcome the limitations which disturb harmony so that he can increase his understanding and sympathy for his fellow men. Peace is born in the purity of the heart. Sufism points the way to that ideal. May this book make its own contribution to the further spreading of this universal Sufi ideal.

1

The Origin and History of Sufism

The origin of mysticism in the Egyptian mysteries

The name Sufism has been related to the Greek word *sophia*, which means wisdom, and to the Arab word *sof*, which means purity; the latter also refers to the pure white woollen garments worn by certain Sufis. Together these words indicate pure wisdom, the wisdom that arises in the pure consciousness from which all impressions and problems of outer life have been wiped away; the wisdom of the heart, not that of the intellect. Originally, Inayat Khan subtitled his Sufi Order as 'The Order of Purity'. Discipleship, the personal relationship between the spiritual disciple who is searching for truth, the *mureed*, and the spiritual teacher, the *shaikh* or *murshid*, has always been of great importance in mysticism. The spiritual radiance – in silence – can transmit the living essence of truth, the experience of it, much more deeply and purely than explanations in words and theories.

In ancient times spiritual wisdom had been transmitted personally from teacher to disciple and by individual contact with saints and mystics. We can trace the line of this mystical tradition back to very ancient times. European and Islamic views agree in finding the oldest source of such wisdom in the Egyptian mysteries, which found their written expression in the Hermetic scriptures, ascribed to

Hermes Trismegistos (Hermes the Thrice-Greatest, the Greek name for the Egyptian god Thoth). These scriptures are held to have been perpetuated through the so-called Hermetic chain of Pythagorean and Neoplatonic philosophers and mystics. An important link between this old mysticism and Sufism in the time of Islam is the figure of Dhul-Nun al-Misti (AD 830) who, according to the authoritative British Orientalist R A Nicholson – 'above all others gave to the Sufi doctrine its permanent shape.'[1] This Dhul-Nun was a Nubian, an Egyptian Hermetic and Sufi. It is said that he could read the Egyptian hieroglyphs. The ancient Egyptian esoteric knowledge apparently continued under the surface when Egypt was brought under early Christian and later under Islamic influence.[2] Dhul-Nun saw God as expressing himself in the whole universe. This realization of the unity of God is central to mystic and Sufi thought. Dhul-Nun put this into words in the following inspiring prayer:

> O God, I never hearken to the voices of the beasts or the rustle of the trees, the splashing of waters or the song of birds, the whistling of the wind or the rumble of thunder, but I sense in them a testimony to Thy Unity (wahdaniya), and a proof of Thy Incomparableness; that Thou art the All-prevailing, the All-knowing, the All-wise, the All-just, the All-true, and that in Thee is neither overthrow nor ignorance nor folly nor injustice nor lying. O God, I acknowledge Thee in the proof of Thy handiwork and the evidence of Thy acts: grant me, O God, to seek Thy Satisfaction with my satisfaction, and the Delight of a Father in His child, remembering Thee in my love for Thee, with serene tranquillity and firm resolve.[3]

Dhul-Nun then sings about his love of the divine beloved, as Rabia of Basra had done before him and as was to become characteristic of many future Sufis:

I die, and yet not dies in me
The ardour of my love for Thee,
Nor hath Thy Love, my only goal,
Assuaged the fever of my soul.

To Thee alone my spirit cries;
In Thee my whole ambition lies,
And still Thy Wealth is far above
The poverty of my small love.

I turn to Thee in my request,
And seek in Thee my final rest;
To Thee my loud lament is brought,
Thou dwellest in my secret thought.[3]

The Hermetic wisdom, which inspired Dhul-Nun, dates back to the time of the pyramids, around 3000 BC. In Roman times it was known that a secret wisdom was stored by the priests of Egypt. This wisdom was very similar to the later Sufi mysticism. It had the same vision of the unity of God, living in the whole creation, which Dhul-Nun expressed. L Hoyack quotes the following Egyptian text:

God is one and alone, no other is beside Him
God is the one who made everything
God is a spirit, a hidden spirit, the spirit of spirits
God is the eternal
God is hidden and nobody has recognized his appearance
Nobody has found his image. He is hidden for God and humans
Hidden remains his name
God is truth and he lives by truth
Innumerable are his names
God is life and all live by Him
He blows the breath of life into the nose of mankind
God is father and mother
God is the being itself
God has made everything
God is the one who has expressed himself in multiplicity
God is the creator of heaven and earth, the father of the gods
God is compassion, protects the weak, listens to the prayers of

those who have been caught, he is compassionate
He is judge between the powerful and the poor
God recognizes the one who recognizes Him, who serves Him
and protects the one who follows Him.[4]

Hoyack comments that this text could have been quoted from the Old Testament or the Qur'an. And Hazrat Inayat Khan sees a direct initiatory link which he describes in the following way:

> When Abraham returned from Egypt after his initiation into the mysteries of life, he arrived at Mecca; and the stone was set there in memory of the initiation which he had just received from the ancient esoteric school of Egypt; and the voice that was put into it by the singing soul of Abraham continued, and became audible to those who could hear it. The prophets and seers since that time have made pilgrimages to this stone of Ka'ba; the voice continued and is still existing.[5]

The purpose of these early mystics was also to commune, to unify with God. The way to this experience is indicated in a passage by Poimandres (a Greek rendering of the Hermetic text):

> The knowledge that one receives of God, is a divine silence, the closing of all senses; for by losing the consciousness of all sensation, of all bodily movement, the soul (*nous*) remains in repose; and when the beauty of God has poured its light over the soul . . . by this means the whole man is transfigured by her into the essence of being.[6]

This passage suggests a deep mystical experience, entirely corresponding to explanations by Hazrat Inayat Khan to which we will return later. These quotations suffice to show that Egypt had a unique position in ancient religion; it could be seen then as the esoteric heart of humanity. And Hermetism seems the stem of esotericism. Inayat Khan sees evidence of this in the Egyptian pyramid. He states that this architecture had reached a spiritual stage, and he adds: 'It was a mystical age, and everything they did was not done with mechanical power, it was done with spiritual power; and therefore what they have made will last . . .[7]

Influences on Sufism in the world of Islam

Besides the oldest tradition beginning in the Egyptian mysteries and the new impulse from the Qur'anic revelation, which stimulated the search for personal divine communication, we can trace different connections between Sufism and mystical currents in the other great religions which met each other in the Middle East. For Universal Sufism – Sufism as it was renewed and inspired by Hazrat Inayat Khan – these connections are of interest, for it is the easy confluence of different mystical currents into Sufism that demonstrates its essentially universal character. In this context it is fitting to mention the towering figure of Sufi Shihabuddin Yahya al Suhrawardi (1151–91) who in a highly creative and personal way aimed at the integration of all forms of and currents in Sufism into one philosophic and esoteric whole. Essentially, Suhrawardi sought to give spiritual and symbolical elements from both the Hermetic and the Zoroastrian traditions a vital role in Sufism.

The struggle between good and evil, light and darkness, plays an important role in the Zoroastrian religion. Suhrawardi built a mystical philosophy of illumination from its principle of divine light. His best known works are *The Philosophy of Illumination* and *The Temple of Light*. (It is interesting in this context that as a young man Hazrat Inayat Khan felt particularly close to the Parsis, Zoroastrians who were the most modern and advanced social group living at that time in his native Baroda.)

Suhrawardi was searching for a living synthesis based on the perennial mystical tradition, as it was expressed in the course of the centuries, first through Hermes, then by Plato, then by the sages of India and Persia.

In the society in which Sufism has developed, Judaism has a traditional place. It is principally the personality of Moses, the great Jewish prophet, which has inspired Sufis. As Hazrat Inayat Khan says: 'Moses, the most shining prophet of the Old Testament . . . has been the favourite character of the poets of Arabia and Persia, and in the poems of the Persian Sufis Moses is mentioned as often as is Krishna in the poetry of the Hindus.'[8]

Here, the story of Moses' ascent of Mount Sinai is that 'on arriving at the summit he saw a flash of lightning which was so powerful that it went throughout his whole being. Moses fell down unconscious, and when he recovered his senses, he found himself in a state of illumination.'[9] Inayat Khan explains that this shows that 'it can be possible for illumination to come to a soul in a moment'. And 'Moses falling upon the ground may be interpreted as the cross, which means, "I am not; Thou art". In order to be, one must pass through a stage of being nothing. In Sufi terms this is called *fanà*, when one thinks, "I am not what I had always thought myself to be". This is the true self-denial, which the Hindus call *layam*, and the Buddhists call annihilation. It is the annihilation of the false self which gives rise to the true self; once this is done, from that moment man approaches closer and closer to God, until he stands face to face with his divine ideal, with which he can communicate at every moment of his life.'[10]

Christian influences emanated mainly from an Eastern Christianity that was close to Arabic thought and temper. While Christian monks and ascetics, by example and discussion, provided a model for their aspiring Muslim counterparts, there were long and friendly relations between them. The transition from the austere piety and commitment of early asceticism to a full mysticism was effected by the increasing predominance in spiritual consciousness of the love of God. The rise in importance of this crucial element seems to have run through all the various religious traditions of the period. It cannot therefore be said that any one religion became predominant, but the interaction of expression in poetry and aphorisms between these different religious groups must have exerted a valuable stimulus.

Independently from all this the personality of Jesus exerted his influence on ascetic and mystical idealism. In a unique but outstanding case that ideal had a very powerful impact. Mansur Al Hallaj (as he has mostly been known) has remained one of the greatest names in Sufism throughout the centuries. His celebrated phrase *'Ana' al Haqq'* ('I am the Truth' or 'I am God') led to his execution for incitement to heresy in 922. In his proclamations of God becoming incarnate in man, his great example was Jesus, and he consciously and consistently accepted condemnation and suffering as part and price of his divine destiny. It must be admitted, indeed, that he provoked his martyrdom. Like many others, including his own teacher Al Junayd and the extremist, Beyazid Bistami, Al Hallaj would have escaped unharmed if he had not publicized his convictions so loudly, for the caliphal government in Baghdad persecuted such ideologically unacceptable doctrines only when they led to social or political unrest and agitation. He sought to bear witness in an almost Christian sense, testifying insistently. Both the Incarnation and the suffering of Christ were sources of inspiration to him; and, of course, Al Hallaj's saying 'I am the Truth' was the essence of Sufi mysticism. It follows from the realization that truth is God and God is one, omnipresent and all-pervading. It is our identification with our limited personality which makes it impossible for us to unite in our consciousness with the divine being. Once that identification has been destroyed one realizes the unity. Al Hallaj prayed for this: 'Oh Lord, remove by thy self, my "it is I" which torments me.'[11] And when this unification was granted to him he expressed his experience in this *'Ana' al Haqq'*, 'I am God'. But most moving were his noble words at his execution:

Oh Lord, I entreat Thee, give me to be thankful for Thy grace
which You have bestowed on me. You have concealed from
others what you have revealed to me – the glories of Thy shining
countenance. You have made it lawful for me to behold the
mysteries of Thy inner consciousness and made it unlawful for
others. As for these others, Thy servants, zealous of religion,
desirous of Thy favor, who have gathered to kill me, forgive and
have mercy on them for if Thou hadst revealed what Thou hast
hid I should not suffer this. All praise belongs to Thee in
whatsoever Thou dost decree.[12]

Contributions to Sufism from the other main streams of
religious inspiration, Hinduism and Buddhism, are more
difficult to trace. But it is interesting to see how Beyazid
Bistami (9th Century) based his own authentic mystical
experience on the Upanishads. It has been shown that this
relationship was indeed a reality, probably through a Sufi
teacher from Sind well versed in the Vedantic tradition.
Thus, amongst Bistami's ecstatic utterances we find the famous 'Thou art that'; an exclamation, 'Glory to me!', equally
to be traced back to the Upanishads; as well as 'I am He'.[13]
These experiences of the realization of unity with God are
essential to all mysticism. Bistami also uses other Hindu
contributions; thus he introduces an Arabic term for the
concept of *maya*: the illusion of the outer world.

Finally, we know that there was an active Buddhist community in Balkh in eastern Persia (now in Afghan Turke-
stan); and that this city became known later for its Sufis. One
of the most famous of the early ascetic Sufis originated here,
symbolizing in his person the link between the *bhikshu* and
the *zahid*, the Buddhist and Sufi ascetics. This was Ibrahim
B Adham, a prince of Balkh, son of a king of Khorasan. The
legend of his conversion to asceticism has often been compared with the story of Gautama Buddha. While out hunting
he heard a voice saying to him, 'It was not for this thou wast
created; it was not this thou was charged to do'. He looked
and saw no one, and said, 'God curse the devil'. But when

he continued he heard the same voice again more clearly. This was repeated yet again; and then he obeyed the voice of God.[14]

Once Adham was asked for a definition of service and he replied: 'The beginning of service is meditation and silence, save for the recollection of God.'[15] (Meaning the Sufi practice of *dhikr* or *zikar*.) This shows the emphasis the early Sufis put on the inner life.

Sufi poetry

After Beyazid Bistami and Al Hallaj, a further gallery of interesting figures leads on to the 11th-Century teacher, Al-Ghazzali. Then, in the 13th Century, classical Sufism reached its culmination in Ibn al-'Arabi, the Spanish philosopher and mystic, and Maulana Jelal-ud-Din Rumi, the Persian Sufi poet, whose *Mathnavi* forms the poetic counterpart to Ibn al-'Arabi's theoretical work. Sufi poetry flourished in Persia during this period. The poetic imagination of the Persians was a fruitful source for this expression of Sufism. A great number of Sufi mystics preferred to express themselves in poems, stories and literary symbols, because in this way they could avoid giving offence to the Orthodox; and because it was realized that in any event truth can never be put down exactly in theories. As well as Rumi, Farid-ud-Din Attar, Saadi, Hafiz and Omar Khayyám have become known in the West as great poets. A few brief passages from some of these famous Sufi poets can give an idea of the atmosphere of Sufism that inspired Hazrat Inayat Khan, who often quotes these same poets in his teachings.

Jelal-ud-Din Rumi, whose father was a learned theologian, studied Sufism from an early age and himself became a recognized religious teacher. But inner enlightenment came to him through his meeting with Shams e-Tabriz, a dervish, who behaved in a strange and wild manner, but in whom he saw the perfect picture of the divine beloved. For years they were inseparable. Shams e-Tabriz inspired Rumi to reach beyond his study of books; legend says that it was he who threw away the manuscript on which Rumi had been working for years. In this way Tabriz brought him to the inner light, to spiritual love; and in this way Rumi became an inspired poet who in many forms, symbols and stories expressed the glow of love for the divine beloved. He expressed his mystical inspiration also in a whirling dervish dance which was practised by his Mevlevi Sufi order, a mystical dance which has been continued until the present day. Often Rumi wrote his poems while in a state of ecstasy, and for that reason they still are living and an eternal source of inspiration, although they are not always easy to understand. One has to listen to them with the inner ear. A few quotations are the best way to give an impression of the wonderful atmosphere of Rumi's poetry. His most famous work, the *Mathnavi*, begins with the well-known comparison to the flute of reed:

> Listen to the reed how it tells a tale, complaining of separations
>   – saying,
> 'Ever since I was parted from the reed-bed, my lament hath
>   caused man and woman to moan.
> Every one who is left far from his source wishes back the time
>   when he was united with it.
> 'Tis the fire of Love that is in the reed, 'tis the fervour of Love
>   that is in the wine.
> The reed is the comrade of every one who has been parted from
>   a friend: its strains pierced our hearts.[16]

Hazrat Inayat Khan says about this comparison of Rumi:

> By the flute he means the soul; the soul which has been cut apart
> from its origin, from the stem, the stem which is God. And the
> constant cry of the soul, whether it knows it or not, is to find
> again that stem from which it has been cut apart.[17]

And at another place Inayat Khan adds the following explanation:

> Man is a piece of bamboo cut away from its stem;
> that stem is whole, is perfect; the piece is imperfect;
> life has cut holes to its heart that it may sound all the notes. Once
> the holes are made, it begins to give the music that wins the
> souls of men.[18]

In another series of poems Rumi points out the delight of this longing:

> O Sound of the sweet-conversing reed, in your note is the taste
> of sugar; your note brings me night and morning the scent of
> fidelity. Make beginning again, play those airs once more; O sun
> lovely of presence, glory over all the lovely ones!
>
> Be silent, do not rend the veil; drain the flagon of the silent
> ones; be a veiler, habituate yourself to the clemency of God.[19]

The last verse touches on two other important aspects:
1) silence, the flagon of the silent ones that we have to drink; and with which we have to 2) unveil the divine mystery. Another aspect of this veiling is the clemency of God who does not wish to see our shortcomings too much.

The following verse also sings of the silence of the heart:

> If your desire from faith is security, seek your security in seclu-
> sion. What is the place of seclusion? The house of the heart;
> become habituated to dwell in the heart; In the heart's house is
> delivered that bowl of wholesome and everlasting wine. Be
> silent, and practise the art of silence; let go all artful bragging;
> for the heart is the place of faith, there in the heart hold fast to
> faithfulness.[20]

But we have to follow a road, climb a height, in order to touch the heavenly spheres.

> I said, 'Show me the ladder, that I may mount up to heaven'.
> He said, 'Your head is the ladder; bring your head down under
> your feet'.
>
> When you place your feet on your head, you will place your
> feet on the head of the stars; when you cleave through the air,

set your foot on the air, so, and come! A hundred ways to
heaven's air become manifest to you; you go flying up to heaven
every dawning like a prayer.[21]

We have to bow our head, lay down our intellect. In and by
that surrender we can ascend. The heart must be opened;
then we can become one:

> Hark, for I am at the door! Open the door; to bar the door is not
> the sign of good pleasure. In the heart of every atom is a
> courtyard for You; until You unbar it, it will remain in conceal-
> ment. You are the Splitter of Dawn, the Lord of the Daybreak;
> You open a hundred doors and say, 'Come in!' It is not I at the
> door, but You; grant access, open the door to Yourself.[22]

This short selection from the immense richness of Rumi's
poetry can give us a first impression of the fiery warmth of
this old Sufi mysticism.

Another great Sufi poet, Hafiz of Shiraz, was the master of
the Persian *ghazal*, close to our own sonnet, in which he sings
about wine and love; and about forgetting the limited self.
Some short passages from Hafiz' poems give an impression
of the exaltation in these divine love songs:

> Nay, by the hand that sells me wine, I vow
> No more the brimming cup shall touch my lips,
> Until my mistress with her radiant brow
> Adorns my feast – until Love's secret slips
> From her, as from the candle's tongue of flame,
> Though I, the singéd moth, for very shame,
> Dare not extol Love's light without eclipse.[23]

The glow of love makes one wish that the ego should eclipse.
The comparison with the moth, burning itself because of its
love for the candle's flame, is often used in Sufi poetry. This
love is above all earthly gain and loss:

> Look upon all the gold in the world's mart,
> On all the tears the world hath shed in vain;
> Shall they not satisfy thy craving heart?

> I have enough of loss, enough of gain;
> I have my Love, what more can I obtain?
> Mine is the joy of her companionship
> Whose healing lip is laid upon my lip – This is enough
>   for me![24]

What is important is to overcome the limited self:

> Self, Hafiz, self! That must thou overcome!
> Hearken the wisdom of the tavern-daughter!
> Vain little baggage – well, upon my word!
> Thou fairy figment made of clay and water,
> As busy with thy beauty as a bird.
> Well, Hafiz, Life's a riddle – give it up:
> There is no answer to it but this cup.[25]

Another important aspect of Sufism developed in Muslih-ud-Din Saadi's work. His simple stories and comparisons show important spiritual virtues that can be developed in daily life. In this way his accent is on development of the personality. He compares the heart to a flower that blooms in beauty and spreads its perfume. Two well-known works of Saadi are the *Gulistan*, meaning 'rose garden', and the *Bustan*, 'place of perfume'. Gratitude, trust in God and surrender to God are key concepts. In this way he also addresses himself to the king, to governors:

> O King! deck not thyself in royal garments when thou comest to worship; make thy supplications like a *dervish*, saying: 'O God! powerful and strong Thou art. I am no monarch, but a beggar in Thy court. Unless Thy help sustain me, what can issue from my hand? Succour me, and give me the means of virtue, or else how can I benefit my people?
>
>   If thou rule by day, pray fervently by night. The great among thy servants wait upon thee at thy door; thus shouldest thou serve, with thy head in worship upon God's threshold.[26]

This is the ideal attitude for everyone who bears responsibility. Hazrat Inayat Khan quotes a very similar story and relates it to the opening of the heart:

To the extent to which a heart is opened, to that extent the horizon of beauty manifests to his view. It is not only that the awakened heart draws man nearer, but a living heart also draws God closer. It is as in the story of a Persian king, to whom his Grand Vizier said, 'All day long you give your time to the work of the state and at night you are occupied in devotion to God. Why is this?' The king answered, 'At night I pursue God, so that during the day God will follow me!'[27]

Another story from the *Gulistan* of Saadi introduces the great Sufi Dhul-Nun al-Misri, who has been discussed earlier as a link between Sufism and the Egyptian mysteries. Here he expresses the importance of developing a feeling of dependence and fear of God just as real as in relation to an earthly ruler:

> A vizier [a minister] paid a visit to Dhulnun Misri and asked for his favour, saying: 'I am day and night engaged in the service of the sultan and hoping to be rewarded but nevertheless dread to be punished by him.' Dhulnun wept and said: 'Had I feared God, the great and glorious, as thou fearest the sultan, I would be one of the number of the righteous.'

> > If there were no hope of rest and trouble
> > The foot of the dervish would be upon the sphere
> > And if the vizier feared God
> > Like the king he would be king.[28]

We find a different aspect again in the story of a vizier who experienced the blessing of being with dervishes (Sufi mystics) and becomes indifferent to all that a governing position can offer:

> A vizier, who had been removed from his post, entered the circle of dervishes, and the blessing of their society took such effect upon him that he became contented in his mind. When the king was again favourably disposed towards him and ordered him to resume his office, he refused and said: 'Retirement is better than occupation.'[29]

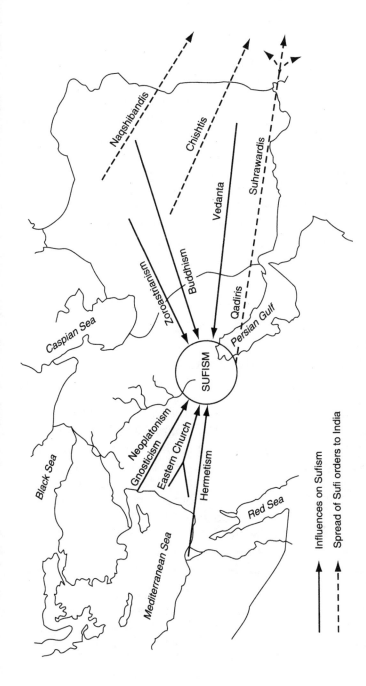

Figure 1 Religious and mystical influences on Sufism

Influences on Sufism

Spread of Sufi orders to India

Voyage of Sufism to India

Sufism spread from Persia and the Middle East in the 13th Century, when Sufis from various Sufi Orders travelled to India. Muslim kings, who had conquered parts of northern India, offered them protection and prestige, but these Sufi missionaries worked individually without backing from any central organization behind them. Through their sincere devoutness and spirituality they attracted many followers. Islamic Sufism found a most hospitable home on Indian soil.[30] India, with its long spiritual background, was very open to this new faith. The first Sufi Order to come to India was the Suhrawardia Order.[31] Many teachers from this Order became the spiritual guides of ruling princes; thus, the Nizam of Hyderabad was a spiritual descendant of the Sufis of the Suhrawardia Order. The largest Sufi Order in India now is the Chishtia Order, which was introduced into India in 1192 by Muin-ud-Din Chishti.

It was to this Order that Hazrat Inayat Khan's initiator, Muhammad Abu Hashim Madani, belonged. Its founder, Muin-ud-Din Chishti, was educated in Bokhara and Samarkand. He was initiated by Hazrat Usman Harooni and travelled with his *murshid* to many places in the Middle East. It is said that during a stay in Medina he had a dream of the holy prophet who told him to go to Ajmer. Chishti did not know where this was; but in another dream he was shown a map marked with the exact position of Ajmer in northern India. He travelled first to Delhi which was then still governed by a Hindu king, Raja Prithwiraja. The governor ordered his expulsion from Delhi. It is told, however, that

> whosoever went to execute the Order, he was so irresistibly over-powered and subdued by the great saint's magnetic personality and affectionate demeanour that he was, on the contrary, obliged to listen to Khwaja Saheb's [Chishti's] sermon and embrace Islam instead of evicting him from the city.[32]

Thus 'Khwaja' conquered the hearts of Indians by his spiritual realization and a message of peace and love. One great attraction of the Islamic Sufi Orders in India was the ideal of brotherhood, recognizing all members as equal without any of the caste distinctions which so characterized and divided Indian society. In Ajmer, in the beginning, Chishti also faced strong opposition; but he was miraculously protected, attracted many followers and established himself there. He wrote illuminating letters to Qutubuddin Bakhtiyar Kaki, his *khalif* (spiritual successor), who was leading the Order in Delhi. In one of these he writes:

> How can one know that one has reached the nearness to God? He [Chishti] replied – 'The best way of knowing it is the doing of good deeds. Know it for certain that on him the door of nearness is opened who is given the power of doing good deeds.'[33]

This was apparently typical of him, for he was very often called *Gharib Nawaz*, meaning the patron of the poor. Another inspiring saying by Chishti, very typical of mystical philosophy, is the following:

> Knowledge is comprised unto an unfathomable ocean and enlightenment is like a wave in it, then what is the relation of God and man? While the ocean of knowledge is sustained by God alone, the enlightenment pertains to man.[34]

Chishti died in 1236 at the age of 93. His *dargah* (the tomb of a saint) in Ajmer has become a sacred place of pilgrimage that still attracts hundreds of thousands of worshippers every year. When visiting this place one is very touched by the light and inspiring atmosphere. In the *dargah* compound the visitor is also impressed by an enormous cauldron, taller than a man, used for cooking food for the poor. This shows again how good deeds – social work – were bound up with spiritual teaching. In the teaching and meditation of the Chishtia Order music plays a very important role. It is told

of Muin-ud-Din Chishti that, listening to music, he sometimes became unconscious in a state of rapture. His musical
concerts stimulated spiritual ecstasy.[35] This musical tradition
continued over the centuries with the Chishtia Order, which
has lived on through a long line of successive spiritual
teachers to the present time.

One of the spiritual descendants of Muin-ud-Din Chishti
was Nizam-ud-Din Aulia (1238–1325), who was buried outside Delhi – in what is now New Delhi. His *dargah*, with the
adjoining mosque and *dargah* of Amir Khusrau, the great
Indian Sufi poet who was his disciple, has also become a holy
place visited by hundreds of thousands of worshippers
every year.

In the later part of the 19th Century Maula Bakhsh, Inayat
Khan's grandfather and a great musician, became the first
director of the Academy of Music (*Gayanshala*) in Baroda. He
was very eclectic and brought together many different currents of Indian music. It was from within this tradition in his
family that Inayat Khan was raised, to become the great
mystic who was destined to universalize Sufism and to bring
the wisdom of Sufism to the Western world. Thus Sufism
continues its voyage.

2

Hazrat Inayat Khan[1]

Childhood

Inayat Khan was born in Baroda, India, on 5 July 1882. Baroda was a progressive state. Its maharaja, Sayaji Rao Gaekwar, described his ideals for India as follows:

India must cease to be an agricultural country and must make her place among the commercial and manufacturing nations. I can conceive of no loftier mission than this; to teach philosophy to the West and learn its science, to impart purity of life to Europe and attain to her loftier political ideal, to inculcate spirituality to the American mind and acquire the business ways of her merchants.

This ideal of bringing together the best qualities of East and West was later to become one of the purposes of Inayat Khan's Sufi movement.

Inayat Khan's maternal grandfather, Maula Bakhsh, played a very important role in his life. Maula Bakhsh received his name from a dervish belonging to the Chishtia Sufi Order, who asked him to sing for him, gave him a blessing and told him: 'Maula Bakhsh, a God-gifted, shall be your name and this name shall be known throughout this land of India and your music shall make it famous' (*B*, p 19).

A few years later Maula Bakhsh was accepted as the sole pupil of one of India's most accomplished singers, Ghasit Khan. He learnt everything from this teacher and stayed with him until he died. Then he started travelling through India, staying at the courts of many maharajas, where he met the highest appreciation of his art. Thus he got to know both the music of northern India – influenced by Persian and Arabic music – and the more austere music of the south, which was held to be sacred and a part of religion. His music began to reflect the skill of the north together with the depth of the south. His aim became to develop a system of notation for music, combining northern and southern practice, so that it should be acceptable in all of India.[2] He also studied Western music – as a preparation for his introduction to the viceroy. When he returned to Baroda after many years, the progressive maharaja founded the *Gayanshala* (Academy of Music) and appointed Maula Bakhsh as its first director. This enabled Maula Bakhsh to devote his life from then until his death in 1896 to the development of and education in Indian music. Under his leadership the Academy was open to all, whatever their caste, creed, sex or from whatever school of music. He felt that music should form the basis of education for every child, because of its influence on character.

Maula Bakhsh's house became a meeting place for philosophers and poets as well as musicians, as the reforms of the maharaja attracted some of the best Indian minds, both Muslim and Hindu, to Baroda. Maula Bakhsh had been brought up as a Muslim, but he recognized the beauty in all religions and many of his pupils were Brahmans.

This was the atmosphere in which Inayat Khan grew up: inspiring music, a universal outlook open to all human beings beyond distinctions and differences, serving all by bringing together the two poles of Indian music. It was only natural that a very close contact developed between Inayat and his grandfather.

It was as if the hungering and thirsting child drew into himself the whole soul of his grandfather and as if the grandfather fostered and watched the child in the belief that here was the most complete fruit of an existence spent in the pursuit of the ideal (*B*, p 29).

When Inayat was a boy, his grandfather used to wake him in the morning and Inayat then spent the morning with him practising, singing and learning music. As he developed, Maula Bakhsh gave more and more attention to him and Inayat's response was such that he absorbed the charm of Maula Bakhsh's personality and all in him that was good and beautiful (*B*, p 44).

Inayat's father, Mashaik Rahmat Khan, also came from a family of musicians, poets and mystics. When he travelled through India he met a teacher and asked him where he should go. The teached waved his hand in the direction of Baroda and so he went there. Rahmat Khan developed a deep and close friendship with Maula Bakhsh; he married his daughter and he helped his father-in-law in his work at the Academy of Music and supported him strongly. Rahmat Khan was the great singer of the classical *dhrupad* music.

As a personality he was strict, but loving and kind. And as the *Biography* puts it: 'Kind actions and courtesy he held to be the chief thing in life and he took pains and every care to spare the feelings of others' (*B*, p 31). Of Inayat's mother, Khatidja Bibi, the *Biography* speaks little but suggests a woman with a subtle, shining personality who was devout, loving and gentle. She had wide interests and knew Arabic, Persian and Urdu. She was as kind to the servants as to the children, always keeping a harmonious atmosphere. She did not wish to have a share of her father's property: 'May God bless my children; if they inherited the great quality of my father, rather than a share of his property, that is quite enough. How long will that earthly property last? That which is dependable in life is only one thing and that is the quality of their grandfather; that they can inherit' (*B*, p 33).

Before Inayat's birth his mother had dreams in which she saw Christ coming and healing her; sometimes Muhammad appeared and blessed her, sometimes she found herself in the midst of prophets and saints, as though they were taking care of or receiving her, or were waiting for something or preparing for a time which they had foreknown. By nature devout, modest, humble and unassuming, she told no one of her dreams except Bima, her grandmother, who also was very pious and at that time very aged. Bima said: 'It is good tidings and yet a great burden and responsibility for you as the mother and also for who will be coming. Do not tell anyone about it but ask the protection of God and the help of those you see' (*B*, p 33).

In such a spiritual family and surroundings Inayat Khan grew up as an exceptionally gifted young man. His inclination, his thinking, his ideals and his experience were all preparing him for the great mission of his life. The *Biography* gives a wonderful picture of his life as a boy and young man in India, with many inspiring stories and incidents of his meetings with musicians, mystics and teachers in the fairy-like world of the Indian princes. Many of these stories give an illuminating insight into spiritual life and Sufism. Only a general outline and a few instances can be given here, for example: 'He found the greatest joy in sharing every cake or sweet he had with his brothers or playmates' (*B*, p 37). He had a strong feeling for the sorrows and pain of those around him and would often retreat into solitude, meditating in silence. This mystical tendency showed itself already in his childhood as 'very often in the midst of great activity or excitement, among his relations and friends, Inayat would be quite tranquil and he would seem above all things around him'(*B*, p 41).

From the beginning he came into contact with different religions, was inspired by them and experienced and expressed the essential unity of truth of all religions. This

started when – coming from a Muslim family – he was sent
to a Marathi (Hindu) school, which taught in the language
of the ruling group, and was considered to be most up to
date although the teaching was still very old-fashioned.[3]
Both his grandfather and his father, seeing his spiritual
interest, brought him into contact with many sages and
yogis. Inayat Khan – still a young boy – used to sit quite still,
absorbed in their atmosphere. Meeting Hamsasvarupa, a
very inspiring *swami* (holy man), Inayat felt a strong leaning
towards Hinduism. He loved to study the *Bhagavadgita* and
was equally fluent in the Marathi of the Hindu scholars, in
the Gujarati of his family's many Parsi friends and in his own
home language of Hindustani (now known as Urdu). At the
same time he was regular in his Muslim prayers and had an
inborn sympathy for Muhammad (*B*, p 53). Later, during his
stay in Hyderabad, he met many Parsis and came into contact with the high priest in this ancient religion of the Zoroastrians, who was enchanted that Inayat 'rendered their sacred
chants into *ragas* with the same enthusiasm and reverence as
he would have his own' (*B*, p 72).

Once, after he had found his own *murshid*,[4] an orthodox
Muslim complained to the *murshid* that 'among his friends
were people of other religions, Hindus, Parsis, Christians
and Jews', but Inayat's *murshid* answered that 'while you see
the outward person of Inayat, I see his inner being. I cannot
very well tell you what Inayat is and what he is to me, except
that he is my beloved *mureed* and I am proud of him' (*B*, pp
77, 78).

Inayat was also strongly interested in the life of the West.
He liked to read about it and also learned English. As soon
as he knew a little of the language he liked to practise it with
any English people he met. He also learned about European
music from his uncle, Alaoddin Khan (Dr A M Pathan), who
had studied in London at the Royal Academy of Music. All
this helped to prepare Inayat for the great mission of his life
in the Western world.

Inayat's father taught him many things of great value. As he saw that Inayat had a strong tendency towards a solitary and ascetic life within nature, he brought about balance by showing him the importance of life in the world. 'For the world is created for some purpose' (*B*, p 55). He showed Inayat the beauty of loving and serving one's fellow man. He taught him to speak the truth and to live a pure life, and he taught him to trust in God. This teaching 'went through the very depths of Inayat's being. It was as though something that was in his nature were brought to the surface' (*B*, p 56).

In 1896, just after Inayat's fourteenth birthday, Maula Bakhsh died. Losing his grandfather, who had such a magical personality, who understood Inayat so well, who was at the same time his friend and his teacher, was a great shock to Inayat. This 'great pain of separation opened his heart wider to the question of birth and death' (*B*, p 58).

First travels through India

His parents felt that a change in Inayat Khan's environment would help him to overcome his grief. They allowed him to accompany his father, at the invitation of the Maharaja of Nepal, to an assembly of eminent Indian musicians.

This was the beginning of Inayat's travels through India. In the course of the following 14 years a number of successive tours brought him all over the Indian continent. The map on the facing page shows the extent of these travels. The description of them in the *Biography* gives them a fairy tale quality. There was the beauty of the Indian natural world. On the first trip to Nepal they travelled through the forest for six days, without any trail. Sedan chairs were sent to carry the guests of the Maharaja through the forest but Inayat preferred to walk, enjoying the beauty of nature, the solitude of the forest, the sounds of the birds. The trees,

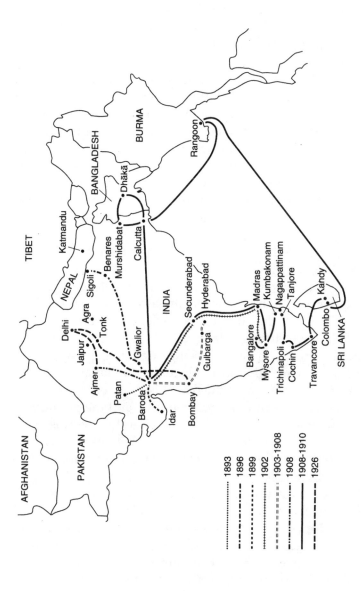

Figure 2   Inayat Khan's travels in India

standing in stillness for hundreds of years, in a place never occupied by man, gave him a feeling of calm and peace. 'He saw the hand of God blessing in every bending branch' (*B*, p 59).

These voyages were particularly important for Inayat's musical and spiritual development. In Khatmandu, the capital of Nepal, Inayat had the opportunity to listen to the great singers of India. This helped him in his continuing advance in the science and art of music. He also saw how music could harmonize the personalities of the musicians; and he learned more than ever to regard music as sacred. But at the same time he saw that 'those who were not yet deepened in music were on the contrary more inclined toward amusement and frivolity, more drawn toward the gaiety and merriment of life, uncontrolled in their affections, and inconsiderate in passion' (*B*, p 61).

He also disliked the tendency of many musicians to praise and flatter their patrons the maharajas in order to gain their favour. He saw that this led to a degeneration in Indian music. Indeed, during a later visit to Bombay in 1902, he found that Indian music was being degraded, giving way to an inclination for light music. He understood that the reason for this was 'that for ages the real music had only been sung chiefly in palaces and rarely in temples, and the public was always kept ignorant of it' (*B*, p 66). Therefore he was often disappointed by his audience's lack of response to his own music. In such a case he learnt to sing to himself; and in that way he was successful.

After about a year Inayat returned to Baroda with his father. His mother welcomed him with joy and mother and son developed a very close contact and mutual understanding. It was a heavy blow, therefore, when his mother died unexpectedly after a brief illness. Inayat then started travelling on his own and was invited to sing at the courts of different maharajas. He had a great success in Mysore and reached the peak of his musical career in Hyderabad, where he hoped to sing for the ruler, the Nizam. After waiting patiently for six months, practising and writing a book on music, a friend introduced him to the prime minister, who was greatly impressed by Inayat and presented him to the Nizam. Here Inayat came in contact with a ruler who understood and appreciated his music and spiritual atmosphere. The *Biography* describes Inayat's meeting with the Nizam as follows:

> When Inayat arrived in the Nizam's presence, the first meeting of glance created an understanding between them. The Nizam, himself a poet and a musician, felt the call that came through Inayat in the realm of music. Inayat at the same time was impressed by the simplicity and kindness and by the unique understanding of human nature that the Nizam had. The Nizam sensed that the musical talent, shown by Inayat, was but an outer garb, covering some wonderful secret, which he sought to fathom (*B*, p 70).

When asked about it, Inayat explained the magic of his music in this way

> as sound is the highest source of manifestation it is mysterious in itself. And whosoever has the knowledge of sound, he indeed knows the secret of the universe. My music is my thought and my thought is my emotion. The deeper I dive into the ocean of feeling, the more beautiful are the pearls I bring forth in the form of melodies. Thus my music creates feeling within me even before others feel it. My music is my religion, therefore worldly success can never be a fit price for it and my sole object in music is to achieve perfection (*B*, p 70).

The Nizam was deeply impressed. He bestowed upon Inayat the name *Tansen*, after the famous singer at Akbar the Great's court, and put a magnificent emerald ring on his finger. This made Inayat known over the whole of India, since the court of Hyderabad was the foremost in the country. After this he was invited to sing everywhere, although at first he stayed only with the Nizam. During his later tours he performed his music in many princely courts of India.

From the very beginning Inayat had taken the opportunity to visit holy places during his travels and to meet with the great Sufis and teachers. In Khatmandu he had discovered an old Sufi with a most beautiful personality. One day while on horseback in the hills

> he saw at a distance someone sitting in a place where scarcely anyone would ever be seen. On arriving there he found the man was a *mahatma*, sitting in silent meditation in that lonely spot, perhaps for ages. In the meeting of glances Inayat was filled with a feeling of exaltation, and the calm and peace and the atmosphere that the *mahatma* had created there were beyond expression. It seemed as if there all the trees, even every leaf, was standing respectfully, motionless before the *mahatma*. It seemed as if the ever-blowing wind was in abeyance under the reign of perfect stillness, caused by the peace of his soul. Inayat sang to that *mahatma* and received in return a blessing through his inspiring glance. After that Inayat frequented the place, sometimes with his *vina*,[5] and won the favour of the *mahatma*. The light, strength and peace that Inayat received from him, designed the career which was destined for him (*B*, pp 62–3).

Inayat Khan's spiritual search

Later, during his stay at the court of the Nizam of Hyderabad, Inayat began to devote more and more time to contemplation. He used to wake up during the night to meditate and he began to feel a radiant light around him. Later it was a voice, 'Allah ho akbar, God is great', which awakened him during the night. He then rose and sat in silence for hours. On one occasion he 'saw with closed eyes a figure rising before him and beheld a most beautiful face. Next day Inayat spoke of his inner experience to his friend, who told him: "Now you have reached a point where you should look for a *murshid*" ' (*B*, p 73).

So he started to search for a teacher. At first several saints whom he approached declined to guide him, showing him instead the greatest respect. Then he visited a great teacher in Hyderabad, *maulana* Khair-ul-Mubin, for whom the Nizam himself would stand reverently in a corner to hear him preach. Even the *maulana* said: 'I? I do not deserve that privilege. I am not worthy'. He had seen in Inayat's eyes what the latter did not express in words, a feeling of reverence, answering which he said: 'I am your servant, your slave' (*B*, p 75). But then, as the *Biography* goes on to tell us:

> By a most wonderful coincidence he received a telepathic message, whereupon he called a boy to open the door and prepare a seat, and turning to his visitors he said: '*Hazrat* [Master] is comimg.' In a moment there appeared, entering in at the door, a personality which seemed as of one who had dropped from heaven and was now gently stepping on the earth, that was not his place. Yet Inayat felt that the face was not unknown to him. On further thought it flashed into his mind that it was the same face which he used to see in his mediation. After the Master had seated himself in the seat prepared for him, he looked at Inayat and it seemed as if he could not take his eyes away from him.
>
> Their glance meeting awakened in an instant, so to speak, an affinity of thousands of years. 'Who is this young man? He attracts my soul very intensely,' said the Master. The *maulana* said: 'Your Holiness, this young man is a musical genius and is desirous of submitting himself to your most inspiring guidance.' The Master instantly granted the request and initiated Inayat then and there.
>
> Inayat wrote a song to his *murshid*, the meaning of which was:

> > Thou hast my hand, my revered initiator,
> > Now my pride is in Thy hand.
> > The heart, my only treasure, I gave Thee,
> > Now nothing is left with me, I am glad.
> > The bowl Thou gavest me made me drunken.
> > Now I ask not for nectar.

> As Joseph Thou didst win my heart,
> As Christ Thou raisest me from the dead,
> As Moses Thou didst give me the Message,
> As Muhammad Thou gavest me the bowl,
> By Thy favour Inayat hath all he desired,
> Hallowed be Thou, Saviour, my Lord.

He sang it to his *murshid*, who was very deeply impressed by it. Thereupon he placed his hands upon Inayat's head and blessed him, saying: 'Be thou blessed by the Divine Light and illuminate the beloved ones of Allah' (*B*, pp 75–6).

From then on a very deep disciple–teacher relationship developed between Inayat and his *murshid*, Sayyed Muhammad Abu Hashim Madani. Inayat went to him as often as he could and 'used to sit in the presence of the *murshid* with open heart, as an empty cup, into which might be poured the illuminating words, the intoxicating glance and the uplifting atmosphere with which the whole surroundings of his *murshid* were charged' (*B*, p 76).

Returning home he remained silent for hours. And when he was with his *murshid* he found that

all problems were solved without Inayat having to ask about anything. Inayat found that words were not necessary, the presence of the *murshid* was itself light which illuminated the minds of those in his presence. All that seemed difficult and obscure became simple and most clear. It seemed as if all were known to him, yet veiled from his eyes and that all became unveiled in the presence of his *murshid* (*B*, p 80).

His friends saw a remarkable change in him, he became quite a different person. His singing also changed. The Nizam marvelled at it and tried to keep him at his court but Inayat began to long for freedom. He had now found something that was so much greater than the worldly grandeur of the court.

When in 1908 his *murshid* departed from this earthly plane – having asked forgiveness from all around him, having prayed for them and having given them his blessings – he

left an aching void in Inayat's heart. The splendid court of
the Nizam did not attract him any longer. So he left and
started on a pilgrimage to the holy men of India. The map
on page 25 shows the extent of this last stage in his travelling.
Once again he met many teachers and Sufis. He was deeply
inspired by his visit to the tomb of Muin-ud-Din Chishti,
founder of the Chishtia Sufi Order in Ajmeer, to which his
murshid had belonged. In the night, listening to the song of
a fakir, he was moved to tears.

> Sitting on his rug with a rosary in his hand, he reflected that all
> the proficiency and reputation which he had achieved were
> utterly profitless in regard to his *najat* or salvation. He recog-
> nized that the world was neither a stage set up for our amuse-
> ment, nor a bazaar to satisfy our vanity and hunger, but a school,
> wherein to learn a hard lesson. He then chose quite a different
> path to the track which he had followed until then, in other
> words he turned over a new page in his life (*B*, p 86).

He wondered what he should do:

> 'Shall I become a dervish and live on the alms offered to me? If
> I did so [he thought] I would only be a burden on those who
> earn their livelihood.' He thought, 'If I went to earn my liveli-
> hood in the world and sold my music for money, it would be
> worse than slavery; besides it would be throwing pearls before
> swine.' To see the music and his profession so badly treated by the
> rich in his country, wounded his heart. He thought that the best
> use he could make of this wound was to try to raise, by his
> independent spirit, the music of India to its pristine glory (*B*, p 89).

So he travelled and gave concerts and lectures about music in
many places. But 'music was his external garb. His life was to
see all day the fakirs and dervishes and to sit for the greater part
of the night in his vigils and to sing at dawn the songs of devotion
and to meditate with music in the evenings' (*B*, p 107).

There were many wonderful and inspiring meetings. One
day he visited a Brahman who was a great seer. When they
were alone the Brahman said to Inayat:

'You are to go to the Western world . . . And there you will do a great work which cannot be told to you just now. It will not bring wealth, but it is work which is beyond imagination. Therefore, build up your courage and all clouds will be cleared away' (*B*, p 109).

Inayat had now reached the culmination of his spiritual search. He could achieve the state of *samadhi* in an instant. As the *Biography* describes:

No sooner did he begin his music than he would rise above the spheres of the earth. It developed to such an extent that not only he himself, but those sitting around him would become spell-bound and feel exalted, in which Inayat found the fulfilment of his having the talent of music. They did not know where they were, or what they were hearing and could not realize to what sphere they were lifted from the earth. After finishing his music Inayat was drowned in ecstasy and they all seemed as if lost in a mist.

So music 'had fulfilled its work in his life; now a new era of his life was to begin' (*B*, p 111).

He now understood why a short time previously he had lost all his medals, which had been awarded to him for his musical success. Indeed, in recent years he had lost all those who had guided him: his grandfather, his father and mother, and his *murshid*. He felt that nothing really *belongs* to an individual. Now his *murshid*'s saying stood out clearly in his consciousness: 'Fare forth into the world, my child, and harmonize the East and West with the harmony of thy music. Spread the wisdom of Sufism abroad, for to this end art thou gifted by Allah, the most Merciful and Compassionate' (*B*, p 111).

So the final preparations were made; the time for his mission had come. Nobody kept him back; a way was cleared; and on 13 September 1910, he left India for the United States. The elder of his two surviving brothers, Maheboob Khan, and his cousin, Muhammad Ali Khan, went with him. He trusted in the divine guidance and protection. In his later autobiography he wrote: 'I was transported by destiny from the world of lyric and poetry to the world of industry and commerce . . . I bade farewell to my mother-land, India, the land of the sun, for America, the land of my future' (*B*, p 121).

His work of spreading the Sufi Message in the Western world had begun.

3

The Sufi Voyage to the West

Seeing the Statue of Liberty when he sailed into the harbour of New York, Inayat Khan felt that it was 'awaiting the moment to rise from material liberty to spiritual liberty' (B, p 123).[1]

Having arrived in New York he was struck by the feeling of being in a totally different world; a world of enormous activity where 'everything seemed moving' (B, p 123). But by bringing the message of unity, he trusted that he would be able to attune himself to the people and conditions.

He came to carry the Sufi message; but he felt that in the beginning his only means was his music, his profession and in this he was helped by his brother, Maheboob Khan, and his cousin, Muhammad Ali Khan, who were also accomplished Indian musicians. Indeed, music opened the first doors to them; they received invitations to give concerts and to talk about Indian music, first at Columbia University in New York and later on the west coast at UCLA and Berkeley. In this way they began to make contacts. But they felt that their music 'was put to a hard test in a foreign land, where it was as the old coins brought to a currency bank' (B, p 123).

With reference to his real aim to bring the Sufi message to the West, he understood that the time was not yet ripe. First he needed time to study the Western world and the psychology of its people to find out how he could fulfil his mission. He found his work in the West 'the most difficult task that he could have ever imagined' (*B*, p 179).

There were many reasons for this.

In the first place he had no organization behind him for support; also he came to a very different world and one in which he had neither acquaintances nor supporters. In this situation there was often a lack of money; he wrote later that 'poverty proved to be my bitterest enemy' (*B*, p 185). For although he records that there were 'several occasions which offered me [the opportunity of] enormous wealth' (*B*, p 185), these did not fit in with his principles. He chose to renounce that profit, feeling that he gained greater strength by keeping to his principle of complete freedom and independence. He explained his attitude about this further in the following words:

> Many wondered if it was beyond the power of a mystic to attract wealth, if he sorely needed it as I did in my life. I could not very well answer this question, but I never felt that it was beyond my reach to obtain wealth if I wanted to. But in this respect my life has been that of a bird, who must descend on earth to pick up a grain, but his joy is in flying in the air. If one told the bird, 'There are no grains in the air, stay on the earth and collect grains', he would say, 'No, it is only a few grains which I need. If there be tons of grains lying on the earth, it will not attract me enough to give up my joy of flying in the air.' In the same way I could not sacrifice the real interest of my life even if all the wealth that the earth can give was offered to me (*B*, p 185).

Beyond this material problem were the difficulties inherent in the prevailing mentality in the West at that time. He met much prejudice: against Islam – even though he was bringing a universal message; against Eastern philosophy and values; even, in some places, a certain colour prejudice; he found that many people were afraid of mystical, psychological or occult ideas (*B*, p 180); and, of course, nationalist feelings became very strong during the First World War.

Finally, his experience was that Western men, even if impressed by the Sufi ideal, found great difficulty in understanding and developing the concept of discipleship, which is so essential on the mystical path. He found that 'in the West there are no disciples, there are teachers'. Even those 'who try to show the disciple-spirit somehow fail to play this role some time or the other' (*B*, p 187). Women understood and sympathized with his work and the Sufi message more readily, being more responsive by nature; and also being less absorbed in working in the world. Women have therefore played a very important role in Inayat Khan's work for the Sufi message. Thus, his first gifted *mureed* and helper in the United States was a woman: Ada Martin, to whom later was given the Sufi name Rabia. When Inayat Khan left for England in 1912, he gave her a high-level initiation and entrusted her with 'the care of a grain of the Message' in America.

Still he felt that he had not yet been able to do much for the furthering of the Sufi movement. Rather, it had been a time of study and adjustment and of making the first contacts. But what was most important was that 'he found the soul who was destined to be my life's partner' (*B*, p 126). He felt that he needed 'the experience of home life, especially with children, with their different stages of development, which gives a complete idea of human nature' (*B*, p 183). Ora Baker was one of his music students. She was strongly attracted to him; and he received an intimation in his meditations that she was meant to be his wife. At first her family prevented her following him to England; but she found a way to follow him and they married in London in 1912 (*B*, p 184). They had four children: two sons – Vilayat and Hidayat, who were to play important roles in continuing the Sufi work later; and two daughters – Noor-un-nissa and Khair-un-nissa. Noor-un-nissa became a heroine of the French resistance movement during the Second World War. She sacrificed her life in a very noble manner.

During the next stage of Inayat Khan's Sufi voyage in

England, it remained difficult for him to make much progress with his mission. He made some interesting contacts but found little response to his music. On being told that there would be more interest in France, he moved to Paris in 1913. Here he made a number of friends who were very open to Indian music and he came to know Claude Debussy, the great composer, who – he noted – 'became very much interested in our ragas'. These seem to have inspired some of Debussy's later compositions.[2]

During his stay in France Inayat Khan was offered the chance to visit Russia. However, he found the experience an uncongenial one: he and his brothers were expected to play their music for the entertainment of the wealthier classes of Russia:

> It was as though God wanted to show me, before disaster [the Revolution] came upon Russia, how even nations are led to destruction when they of their own will choose that path. Had I known beforehand what the offered engagement was, I would certainly not have accepted it. However, God's glory is everywhere to be found (*B*, p 135).

Notwithstanding the inauspicious beginning, the trip became a success. He was invited to the Imperial Conservatory of Music, where the response was extremely enthusiastic (*B*, p 135). He made many friends, especially Serge Tolstoy, son of the famous writer. He found a great interest in religious and philosophical subjects. His first book *A Sufi Message of Spiritual Liberty* was translated into Russian and published there. He also met and became friendly with the Russian composer Skriabin, who felt that 'there was much in the East which could be introduced into the music of the West' (*B*, p 138). Inayat Khan agreed and hoped that in the end such music 'would become a world music, helping to unite humanity' (*B*, p 138).[3]

By the time he left Russia in 1914 Inayat Khan had become attached to the country and its people. He liked their language, which seemed to him similar to Hindustani; he saw an idealism in them and a leaning towards art, mysticism and philosophy. At a meeting in the house of the Muslim leader in Moscow he spoke on brotherhood and had a great response from people from many eastern countries. For him it was 'a vision of home and yet not home' (*B*, p 138).

He returned to Paris in 1914 to participate in a musical congress. Shortly after that the First World War started and he and his family moved back to London where they spent the war years. This was a difficult time. An anecdote from the *Biography* shows how he was given divine help in time of need.

> One day the *murshid* arrived in a town at an unexpected hour, and found nobody at the station to receive him. No lights were to be found in the streets during the time of war, nor was a vehicle to be found. The *murshid* was left alone with all his things to carry, his hands full of bags and his instrument. He walked along the road, expecting to find someone who could show him the way. He saw at a distance men coming. As he approached he found that they had all drunk and were at the moment of their greatest glory. They were laughing aloud. Shouting, fighting and dancing, they came near to the *murshid* where he was standing, loaded with all his bags in the dark. As they approached, one saw the *murshid* and said, 'Oh, who is that?' And in answer to this came out from everyone a burst of laughter. And the *murshid*'s glance fell on them like lightning and it seemed as if all their intoxication and feeling of gaiety vanished in a moment. Then he asked them for the place he was searching after and they said, 'We will take you to the place'. One man took the *murshid*'s bag, a second another bag and a third one also something, but Murshid would not give anyone his *vina*, but two took it away from him with all the force they had and walked on the way as quietly as if they were on their sacred duty. There was not the slightest sign of intoxication left. Everyone of them seemed to have been controlled by some impression within him, which he himself did not realize till the moment they escorted the *murshid* (*B*, pp 259–60).

Inayat Khan felt that 'the war had paralysed people's minds'

The MESSENGER.

N assembly, quietly seated, waiting in a long lofty room ; some with still hands folded and downcast face ; some gazing steadfastly before them, expectant-eyed ; others in whom curiosity, waiting too, was held in abeyance as if restrained by a power that lived, bodiless, in the fragrance of incense that moved around and above, but invisibly.

It was a moment in which one dared breathe but very softly, fearful of disturbing some unknown presence.

Amethyst cinerarias leaned pensively from fired-blue pottery set here and there on small tables about the room.

Soundlessly awaited, he of whom all desired the sight came without sound in a robe of pale gold ; on his breast a winged jewelled heart shone reposefully.

His face was a cradle of peace ; tranquility spread out from him like a radiance that is felt only by the soul. All beautiful thoughts seemed to go home to rest in him.

He came with a message of Love, Harmony, and Beauty. Indeed, he himself was his own message—he typified all that he came to teach.

For a moment he stood in rapt concentration, seeking touch with the Infinite. And then the stillness was wonderfully charmed with the exquisite cadence of a low, mystical chant.

Suddenly he ceased his prayerful song and opened wide, shining eyes upon the gathering, shedding a benediction of intimate happiness.

Slowly he raised a caressing hand, " Beloved ones of God," he said.

F.G.P.W.

From "Southern Daily Echo," Southampton, April 9, 1919.

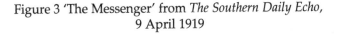

Figure 3 'The Messenger' from *The Southern Daily Echo,* 9 April 1919

(*B*, p 139). The focus was on the war and 'the voice of peace was a dissonant chord to the ears of many' (*B*, p 139). Nevertheless some series of lectures were arranged for him, though he often spoke to very small audiences.

It was during this period that some very devoted *mureeds* came to him. He speaks particularly of a Miss Goodenough 'who stood as a foundation stone for the building of the Order' (*B*, p 141). In her he found a spirit of discipleship, so rare in the West. A Mrs Sainsbury Green was also of great help, especially in creating the Universal Worship activity. The work of spreading the Sufi message was gradually beginning: the first books were published; the Sufi Order was legalized and some Sufi centres were established. Nevertheless Inayat Khan felt that the time 'was [still] given to the tilling of the ground'.

After the war ended in 1918 Inayat Khan felt that conditions in England turned from bad to worse: 'hearts became cold by the later effect of the war' (*B*, p 147). He therefore moved the international headquarters of the Sufi movement from England to Geneva in Switzerland and settled himself with his family near Paris in France, where he felt most at home. From there the work for the Sufi message began to flourish. After a decade of preparation in the West an incredible stream of inspired teachings now began to pour forth from him. This developed in the establishment of his summer schools in Suresnes, in lecture tours through many European countries and in two further trips to America.

In 1923 he found that the great difficulty in the United States 'was to make the Message audible, for I felt as though blowing a whistle among the noise of a thousand drums'. Things should be brought forward 'in a grand manner' (*B*, p 175), otherwise it is difficult to get a response. On his second visit his organization was better; he saw many journalists and gave his first lecture at the Waldorf Astoria Hotel in New York before a large crowd. He described his impressions of this meeting:

'Some of them came from the advertisements, some of them from the reports the newspapers gave, some of them came to see some phenomena performed on the platform, some out of curiosity; and some had the patience to stay there five minutes after they entered the hall. Nevertheless it was a success. It made me wonder as to what the world wants: truth or falsehood. Souls unconsciously seek for truth, but are delighted with falsehood.' (*B*, p 205).

Nevertheless much was accomplished on this trip. Indeed, when we look at the teachings given in those years, their comprehensiveness, depth and clarity is astounding. Whatever the subject in philosophy, psychology, mysticism and religion, Inayat Khan always inspires and points to the essence, the divine spirit. Many *mureeds* were initiated in these years; national societies and centres of the Sufi movement were created and the international headquarters of the Sufi Movement was incorporated in Geneva in 1923.

With all this, Inayat Khan's work load became so heavy that he had to give up his music, a great sacrifice. He explained this decision:

I gave up my music because I had received from it all I had to receive. To serve God, one must sacrifice the dearest thing, and I sacrificed my music, the dearest thing to me. I had composed songs, I sang, and played the *vina*, and practising this music, I arrived at a stage where I touched the music of the spheres. Then every soul became for me a musical note and all life became attracted by my words, listened to them instead of listening to my songs. Now if I do anything, it is to tune souls instead of instruments; to harmonise people instead of notes. If there is anything in my philosophy, it is the law of harmony with oneself and with others. I have found in every word a certain musical value, a melody in every thought, harmony in every feeling, and I have tried to interpret the same thing with clear and simple words to those who used to listen to my music. I played the *vina* until my heart turned into this same instrument; then I offered this instrument to the divine Musician, the only Musician existing. Since then I have become His flute and when He chooses He plays His music. The people give me credit for this music which in reality is not due to me, but to the Musician Who plays on His own instrument.[4]

At the end of his life, when he had returned to India, Hazrat Inayat Khan expressed the wish to be buried near the grave of Nizamuddin Aulia in Delhi. After his death this was done and the international Sufi movement has in recent years been working to improve and expand his *dargah* in India. A marble memorial of exquisite beauty has been built. In the pure and inspiring atmosphere of this *dargah* regular meditations and concerts are organized; at the same time social programmes have been organized for the poor people who are living in this area.

The beauty and harmony of this newly developing *dargah*, against the background of the old Nizam-ud-Din Aulia *dargah*, shows both the continuity of the mystical link through the centuries and the new divine impulse and inspiration of the universal Sufi message that Hazrat Inayat Khan has brought to the Western world.

This brief factual description of Inayat Khan's journeys in the West to teach Universal Sufism is, of course, unable to evoke the spiritual atmosphere of his teachings. A more personal approach seems needed for this. In the next section I will evoke, briefly, the personal experience of some *mureeds* who participated in Inayat Khan's summer schools.

Personal reminiscences of Inayat Khan

Many accounts, many memories tell us of the unforgettable, transforming impression Pir-o-Murshid Inayat Khan made on his disciples, his *mureeds*. Let us start with Azmat Faber, who describes how, in 1923, she was invited by a friend to go to Geneva to meet Murshid Inayat Khan, At the time she was in Switzerland to regain her health and to sort out personal problems. She writes:

I shall never forget these autumn days in Geneva; they were the beginning of a great change. A change that started from the moment that I sat down opposite Murshid in my first interview and when he cast his deep soft glance on me. Words are unable to tell what this first meeting with Murshid meant to me. I was touched by something which I had been longing for in the deepest part of my being. I felt that there was nothing that this man would not understand and that he knew the deepest longing of my soul. All the searching of the last years, the sadness and the loneliness disappeared; it was as though a soft hand took away everything that had disturbed me and caused me pain. It was as though life started anew. In the same week I was initiated by Murshid. Murshid asked me to stay in Geneva so that I would be able to follow the Sufi classes at the Headquarters and could help a little with the work that had to be done. He felt how great was my spiritual hunger and knew that I would find all the possibilities there to deepen myself in Sufism.

When Murshid came again to Geneva in the next Spring, it happened that he gave me another name. Accidentally I did not hear that name directly from Murshid but one of the workers at Headquarters told me about it really by mistake. On that day I did not see Murshid and so I could not ask him for the meaning of this name. The next morning, when I woke up, I repeated for myself softly that name and every time I added: 'I will grow in the glory of God, I will be filled with the glory of God'. And I repeated this several minutes. I was excessively happy, it was as though blessings streamed to me from all sides. Yet, at that moment, I did not understand the relation of all this. Later on the day, however, it became clear. After luncheon Murshid walked with some of his *mureeds* to Headquarters and suddenly he said laughing to me: 'They have spoiled my secret, they have told you your name'. Somebody then asked: 'What does it mean?' And Murshid answered: 'It means God's glory'. What happened that morning was clear to me then, I had repeated the meaning of that name continuously without knowing it. How was that possible, how had that happened?

It was a precious time, this first Summer School. When I finally left and took leave of Murshid, I felt that I had experienced something the scope of which I could scarcely understand. I said to Murshid: 'For me it is as a dream'. To which Murshid answered: 'But it is a dream'. And the way in which Murshid said this made me feel even more deeply how the whole of life is a voyage from imperfection to perfection from something unreal to the real . . .

The last Summer School of 1926 was a climax of beauty. Sometimes it was as though Murshid's whole being radiated light. This especially struck me often on Sunday, the day after the evening when Murshid had given us his blessing in the silence of his *samadhi*. I do not think that it is possible to describe these *samadhi* evenings. They were the most uplifting moments that a human being can experience on earth. Sitting silently in that powerful atmosphere of the divine, before we one by one were allowed to come for a few minutes in Murshid's presence. The glance which Murshid cast at us, the liberating feeling of purification, surpassing everything, it is all difficult to describe. Many of us have felt that last summer in Suresnes as a culmination of all that Murshid could give to us.[5]

Sirkar van Stolk, who accompanied Inayat Khan on many of his European travels, describes a very interesting conversation with Inayat Khan after one of his lectures:

'Did you think that my whole work consists of the giving of lectures?' Murshid went on. 'Those lectures are no more than a screen; my real task lies in the higher spheres. If I had to judge the results of all I do from the attendance of this handful of people, I should feel very discouraged indeed. It is true that I can read what the problems and difficulties are of the souls in my audience – and I try to answer these questions. But as for my real purpose . . . One of the most important tasks I have to fulfil is the tuning of the inner spheres in the different countries I visit, to a higher pitch of vibration. That is why I have to travel so much'[6]

Van Stolk also recalls the following episode:

Even the most practical and critical of men were impressed by Hazrat Inayat Khan; and I shall never forget his meeting with my own father. In the early years of my life, Father had hoped that I would succeed him in the family business; but after I had met Murshid I told him this was no longer possible. I wanted to follow a spiritual path. Although he was deeply disappointed, Father accepted my decision with a remarkably good grace. It was natural, however, that he should want to meet the man who had so profoundly influenced his son; and it was partly for this reason that I arranged, on our return from Germany in 1924, that Murshid should stay for a few days at our house in Holland.

Father was not at all a mystic, nor a religious person in the usual sense of the word, but he was a very keen student of men. He often sought contact with anyone of authority on philosophical or spiritual matters who might have something of value to impart; but, since he had a brilliant mind of his own, he was not easily impressed by their ideas. On the first evening of Murshid's stay, Father invited him into his study after dinner. For a long time they remained there together, deep in conversation, while I retired to bed. I started to read; and was still reading hours later when the study door reopened. Father came upstairs to my room, and sat down slowly on the edge of the bed. 'My boy, my boy,' he said, emphasising the words with a beat of the forefinger, 'this Master of yours is the greatest personality I have ever met. Do you know why? Because he is the only one I know who lives what he teaches'.[7]

Munira Nawn, one of the earliest *mureeds* in the United States, describes the influence of another dinner party with Inayat Khan:

I was privileged to dine several times in the home of Hazrat Inayat before I went away. What was probably the supreme blessing of my entire life occurred on one of these unforgettable occasions. I did not know then that the glance of a seer falling upon a person could confer the greatest grace. So, when I chanced to look over, that evening, and meet the glance of my Murshid, I did not even faintly suspect that a divine impression had been made on my ignorant heart. Yet it must have been so, for long years afterward, while doing a certain practise, I suddenly saw again, in memory, my Murshid sitting across from me at dinner, looking at me as He had looked so long ago. Every night, thereafter, I summoned the picture, and one night, as I rested in the benediction of that compassionate glance, a deep stillness fell upon me, and in that blissful instant I realized Whose dinner-guest I had been.[8]

The wonderful and unique atmosphere of Murshid Inayat Khan's presence and teaching during the summer school is evoked in some very atmospheric drawings by Saida van Tuyll van Serooskerken, one of the early disciples. She had been encouraged by Murshid to draw his portrait, but she did not dare to do this at the time. Later she did so from memory. One of these paintings depicts Murshid at dinner with some invited *mureeds*. Saida describes this scene in her memoirs as follows:

Murshid did not talk much but from time to time he addressed somebody in the circle. It was an impressive togetherness and evoked thoughts of the last supper of Jesus Christ. Once my parents had also been invited for dinner on such an evening. My father was a lively talker and he conversed with great joy until he began to feel the totally different atmosphere in this rather exceptional company. My parents had had Murshid in the Netherlands for dinner but they were not *mureeds*. My father gradually became more and more silent and finally he did not talk any longer. When we came home he said to my mother: 'I think that we have been together with a very great one'.[9]

Another picture shows Murshid in a personal interview. A very special drawing was the one of Murshid in the garden in a storm. Saida describes this scene as follows:

On a day, a Sunday, there were a number of visitors from Paris in Wissous[10] in Murshid's garden. It was August and a thunderstorm was threatening. The air became dark and a strong wind came up. Murshid's wife, brothers, children and visitors fled quickly into the big room. I was the last and I just wanted to open the french windows in order to also go inside when I looked around to see whether Murshid also came. What I saw then I will never forget. Murshid was standing quietly as a grand figure, facing the storm or taking it into himself on a low little hill. The dead leaves and dust were flying around him, blown by the wind. His hair was blowing in the wind. He was standing there as a prophet from the Bible, a Moses, an Abraham. He did not notice that I saw him. Inside the visitors and children were talking, outside the contrast of the eternal forces of nature in their greatness with Murshid. This moment remains imprinted within me forever and later I tried to fix it in an aquarelle.[11]

Ratan de Vries Feyens, who later became my wife, had come into contact with Sufism at a very early age, when her parents took her with them to Suresnes in 1926. When she was six years old she was present at Inayat Khan's last Summer School and was impressed very strongly by his radiant personality.

As a child of six years my parents took me with them to Suresnes near Paris in order to attend a Summer School of two months, a meeting of Sufis. A great deal of what has taken place in my life in the years before and after has become a grey past. These months, however, remain very vivid. In the first place the surroundings, the lovely field with apricot and plum trees, the lecture hall, a clear sky, the radiant sun. Then, an atmosphere of feeling at home. However sad, boring, intense or joyful the changing experiences and circumstances in later life may have been, they have been playing consciously or unconsciously against the background of the feeling that originated there; of having found a home in which I was grounded.

In the third place, as a centre of activity, the people with that uplifted expression on their face and their whole being concentrated on Murshid who was the central, spiritually radiating personality who inspired all those present and kept everything in balance. Being a child I felt intuitively that what happened in these two months in Suresnes was part of that great pouring down on earth of the message of Sufism. This feeling was, of course, also awakened by the old Sufi stories which parents told their children. Murshid did not forget these children. Notwithstanding his most demanding task he found time every week to give a children's class for the children of those who participated in the Summer School. This took place every Friday afternoon in the garden of Fazal Manzil, Murshid's house. Apart from practices in speaking or singing Murshid taught us the first principles of meditation by doing concentration games with us. The idea was that one child should empty the mind while the other children concentrated on a certain animal. It was a fascinating game with sometimes more luck than wisdom. I still hear Murshid's voice, saying: well, what was the animal?

The focus on Murshid's trusted personality, the deep seriousness and at the same time the joyful anticipation and pleasure one had in one's own or another's contribution made these children's classes a feast and an unforgettable remembrance.[12]

4

Universal Sufism:
A Message of Spiritual Liberty

As we have seen, Inayat Khan grew up in an environment of pure Sufism and spiritual music. From his earliest days the influences on him were universal. His grandfather brought together elements of the music of northern and southern India, while in the family there was also great interest in Western music. From an early age Inayat Khan was open to the inspiration of different religions. He went to a Maharathi Hindu school and he met with and learnt from teachers and priests of the many different religions represented in India.

It is generally true to say that the Mogul culture with its composite Hindu–Muslim character, in which Inayat Khan grew up, combined Eastern and Western religious streams. The Western line started with Avestan Zoroastrianism, continued through Judaism and Christianity to Islam and included from the earliest times many of the older religious and philosophical values from Ancient Egypt, Greece and Persia. The Eastern stream originated from the Vedic wisdom followed by Brahmanist teachings. It continued with Buddhism expanding into the Far East, encompassing related traditions such as the Taoist and Confucian teachings (in the same way as in India, it related to Jainism); it culminated in the Hinduism Inayat Khan knew and loved so well – and which, in his time, also included the original teachings of the Sikhs, whose *Granth Saheb* again is so closely akin to Sufi ideals.

In a sense, therefore, we can see this Indian culture as a central stream of mankind's spiritual life. From where else could a response to the problem of the secularist Western world better come? Thus, when Inayat Khan had completely assimilated all these strands of religious and spiritual thoughts, and when he had reached spiritual realization, he set out to fulfil his mission 'to harmonize the East and West' and to spread the wisdom of Sufism as his *murshid* had said.

This is well brought out by Inayat Khan's formulation of one of the aims of the Sufi movement, which he created as an instrument for the work of spreading the Sufi message: 'It belongs to the work of the Sufi Movement to interpret the ideas of these poets, to express their ideas in words that can be understood by modern people, for the value of those ideas is as great today as it ever was.'[1]

The author A J Arberry was apparently unaware of Inayat Khan's Sufi message when he wrote in the epilogue to his history of Sufism:

> If the 'intellectual arguments' must of necessity be of a different order from those which satisfied al-Junaid, al-Ghazali, Ibn'Arabi, Jalal al-Din Rumi, it by no means follows that the discipline of body and spirit invented by the Sufi masters will prove inadequate to meet the requirements of the modern and future man.
>
> It is far from useless to look back into the pages of the distant past. Whether we are Muslims or not, we are all surely children of One Father, and it is therefore no impertinence, no irrelevancy for the Christian scholar to aim at rediscovering those vital truths which made the Sufi Movement so powerful an influence for good. If he may have the co-operation of his Muslim colleagues in this research – and signs are not wanting that he will – together they may hope to unfold a truly remarkable and

Sufi Inayat Khan (1882-1927)

Hazarat Inayat Khan

Hazarat Inayat Khan with a group of *mureeds*
(*Drawing by Saida van Tuyll van Serooskerken*)

An interview with Hazarat Inayat Khan
(*Drawing by Saida van Tuyll van Serooskerken*)

Inayat Khan braving the storm
(*Drawing by Saida van Tuyll van Serooskerken*)

inspiring history of high human endeavour; together they may succeed in retracing a pattern of thought and behaviour which will supply the needs of many seeking the re-establishment of moral and spiritual values in these dark and threatening times.[2]

But more is needed than research into the writings of the old Sufi mystics. A living stream is needed to inspire and renew our spiritual life, and this is precisely what Inayat Khan's Universal Sufism brings to us.

Important aspects of the Sufi message are unity and balance. Universal Sufism illuminates the deeper unity of all great religions and builds a unifying bridge between science, philosophy, mysticism and religion. It shows us the way to the unifying and healing depth of our own being, the soul, that connects us to the divine life. It teaches us to aim for balance between this inner life and the ideals and duties in our outer life.

Balance between head and heart, between strength and wisdom, between activity and repose. The emphasis is on humanity; the ideal is love, harmony and beauty in life. The Sufi message is reaching out to the modern Western world: Inayat Khan went out to that world, has been listening to it and his universalised Sufi teachings are the answer to its needs. It explains the one eternal truth in present-day terms, simple yet deep.

In this way Inayat Khan's Sufism can contribute to a synthesis between the worlds of East and West. It is a message of spiritual liberty which does not impose dogma but leaves us free to follow our own way to the truth. Many of these aspects we find in the formal purposes of the Sufi Movement as inspired by Hazrat Inayat Khan:

1. To realize and spread the knowledge of unity, the religion of love and wisdom, so that the bias of faiths and beliefs may of itself fall away, the human heart may overflow with love and all hatred caused by distinctions and differences may be rooted out.

2. To discover the light and power latent in man, the secret of all religion, the power of mysticism, and the essence of philosophy, without interfering with customs or belief.
3. To help to bring the world's two opposite poles, East and West, closer together by the interchange of thought and ideals, that the Universal Brotherhood may form of itself, and man may meet with man beyond the narrow national and racial boundaries.

These words, however, are inadequate to describe the message of Sufism. It is too rich and too deep to be described briefly. Because its essence, the experience of being touched by the divine that transcends thoughts and words, is mystical, its real meaning and value can never be fully captured in words. It has to be experienced. We can best see it therefore as a divine inspiration which opens the door for us to the eternal source of mystical unity with God and the creation.

The most inspiring evocation of the ideals of Universal Sufism and of the Sufi movement is given by Hazrat Inayat Khan in the following passage:

> At the present time the object of the Sufi Movement is to bring about a better understanding among individuals, nations, and races; and to give help to those who are seeking after truth. Its central theme is to produce the consciousness of the divinity of the human soul; and towards this end the Sufi teaching is given.
>
> It is not only the misunderstanding between East and West or between Christians and Muslims which has brought Sufism to the West, but the misunderstandings among Christians themselves and between individuals in general. Sufism, as a school, has come from the East to the West. The Sufi esoteric school has behind it the tradition of the ancient Sufi schools which existed in all the various periods, but the Sufi message has its own tradition. It is more than a school: it is life itself; it is the answer to the cry of the whole humanity.
>
> Sufism is a religion if one wants to learn religion from it; it is a philosophy if one wants to learn wisdom from it; it is

mysticism if one wishes to be guided by it in the unfoldment of the soul. And yet it is beyond all these things. It is the light, it is the life which is the sustenance of every soul, and which raises a mortal being to immortality. It is the message of love, harmony and beauty. It is a divine message. It is the message of the time; and the message of the time is an answer to the call of every soul. The message, however, is not in its words, but in the divine light and life which heals the souls, bringing to them the calm and peace of God.

Sufism is neither deism nor atheism, for deism means a belief in a God far away in the heavens and atheism means being without belief in God. The Sufi believes in God. In which God? In the God from whom he has become separated, the God within him and outside him; as it is said in the Bible, we live and move and have our being in God. That teaching is the teaching of the Sufis.[3]

5

The Philosophy of Sufism

Science and mysticism: Western and Eastern thought

It has always inspired me to see how Hazrat Inayat Khan, as a mystic, has developed a philosophical vision which is, in many respects, remarkably in harmony with insights which modern scientific thought has reached in an analytical way. Mystics and scientists approach the knowledge of creation along diametrically opposed ways. Science is working with ever-sharper analysis and more refined observation; mysticism penetrates immediately to the essence and discovers in a synthesized inner vision the essential nature and interrelationships of creation. The methodologies of science and of mysticism – as also those of Western and Eastern thinking – have become separated since the Middle Ages. Western science has developed a materialistic causal–deterministic theory quite opposite to mystical and religious visions. But in the present extraordinary time in which we live, these lines again converge and begin to touch each other in certain fields. Accordingly, some scientists have found parallels between the vision of earlier mystics and some aspects of modern science, which is becoming more organic, more holistic and begins to see creation as an indivisible dynamic whole. Causality is replaced in modern science by probability. While in classical mechanics the separate parts determine the whole, in quantum mechanics it is the whole that determines the behaviour of the parts. This development was described in 1930 by Sir James Jeans, the astronomer and physicist: 'The universe begins to look more like a great thought than like a great machine.'[1]

The mystical philosophy which Inayat Khan developed along the lines of earlier mystical thinkers corresponds exactly to this modern picture of the universe. Some essential aspects of this convergence are dealt with below.

Vibration

To begin with Inayat Khan sees the whole creation as vibrations:

> All existing things which we see or hear, which we perceive, vibrate. If it were not for vibration, the precious stones would not show us their colour and their brilliance; it is vibration which makes the trees grow, the fruit ripen, and the flowers bloom. Our existence is also according to the law of vibrations, not only the existence of our physical body but also of our thoughts and feelings.[2]

This is also quite in line with the earliest mystical writings of the Hermetics, where the third principle is that 'nothing is still, all moves, all vibrates'.[3]

There are many different kinds of vibrations. Modern science has subjected them to an analysis of a more and more penetrating refinement, with some remarkable results. It shows a universal harmony that has been described as the 'music of the spheres'.[4]

It is easy to understand that *sound* is a vibration. We both see and feel the string of a violin vibrate. In the terms of physics, sound is created when the molecules of a suitable object, such as a violin string, vibrate. The tone is determined by the number of vibrations per second (for example, middle

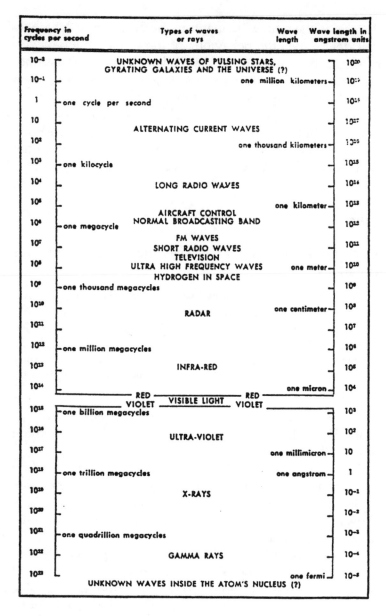

Frequency in cycles per second	Types of waves or rays	Wave length	Wave length in angstrom units
10^{-2}	UNKNOWN WAVES OF PULSING STARS, GYRATING GALAXIES AND THE UNIVERSE (?)		10^{20}
10^{-1}		one million kilometers	10^{19}
1	one cycle per second		10^{18}
10			10^{17}
10^2	ALTERNATING CURRENT WAVES	one thousand kilometers	10^{16}
10^3	one kilocycle		10^{15}
10^4	LONG RADIO WAVES		10^{14}
10^5		one kilometer	10^{13}
10^6	one megacycle	AIRCRAFT CONTROL NORMAL BROADCASTING BAND	10^{12}
10^7	FM WAVES		10^{11}
10^8	SHORT RADIO WAVES TELEVISION ULTRA HIGH FREQUENCY WAVES	one meter	10^{10}
10^9	one thousand megacycles HYDROGEN IN SPACE		10^9
10^{10}		one centimeter	10^8
10^{11}	RADAR		10^7
10^{12}	one million megacycles		10^6
10^{13}	INFRA-RED		10^5
10^{14}		one micron	10^4
10^{15}	RED — VISIBLE LIGHT — RED VIOLET one billion megacycles VIOLET		10^3
10^{16}	ULTRA-VIOLET		10^2
10^{17}		one millimicron	10
10^{18}	one trillion megacycles	one angstrom	1
10^{19}	X-RAYS		10^{-1}
10^{20}			10^{-2}
10^{21}	one quadrillion megacycles		10^{-3}
10^{22}	GAMMA RAYS		10^{-4}
10^{23}		one fermi	10^{-5}
	UNKNOWN WAVES INSIDE THE ATOM'S NUCLEUS (?)		

Figure 4   Chart of radiation spectrum

C is 262 vibrations per second); this is independently of the nature of the vibrating object. Sound is thus – in a sense – an abstract phenomenon. *Light* is a more mysterious vibration. In physics it can be described and analyzed in two ways – as a stream of energy particles (photons), and as a wave. Different colours of light have different wavelengths and frequencies. It is an interesting phenomenon that the product of wavelength and frequency, which is the velocity of light, is always constant at 186,000 miles per second for all kinds of light and radiation.

Visible light, however, is only a small part of the enormous range of electro-magnetic waves. On the lower borders of visible light we have, first, infrared and ultraviolet rays, then a series of radar and radio waves with increasingly lower frequencies; and on the other side, X-rays, with higher frequencies. Figure 4 shows the complex radiation spectrum in its immense range of different frequencies and wavelengths.

Our thoughts and emotions are as invisible as these waves and so far no physical instrument has been able to measure them. Their effect can be observed, however, in psychology and parapsychology. They are vibrations of a different kind, which can be transmitted from one person to another, sometimes over large distances. We observe this in daily life when we feel the mood of another person through his 'atmosphere', without this being expressed in words. The phenomenon of telepathy proves that certain thoughts, directed to a particular person, can be received by him or her even over large distances. As miraculous to our ordinary thinking is the phenomenon of synchronicity, where the same thought can rise simultaneously in the minds of different thinkers who otherwise are not in contact in any way. Inayat Khan points out that finer vibrations reach farther:

> The reach of vibrations is according to the fineness of the plane of their starting point. To speak more plainly, the word uttered

by the lips can reach only the ears of the hearer; but the thought proceeding from the mind reaches far, shooting from mind to mind. The vibrations of mind are much stronger than those of words. The earnest feelings of one heart can pierce the heart of another, they speak in the silence, spreading out into the sphere, so that the very atmosphere of a person's presence proclaims his thoughts and emotions. The vibrations of the soul are the most powerful and far-reaching, they run like an electric current from soul to soul.[5]

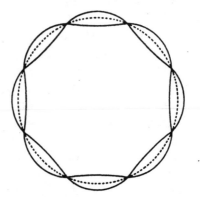

Figure 5   The orbit of an electron

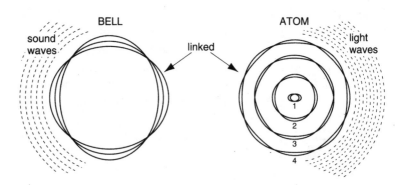

Figure 6   Vibration analogy

Finally we come to the nature of matter, which appears to us as solid and concrete and not in the least like a vibration. But quantum theory has now arrived at the conclusion that matter analyzed to its smallest sub-atomic parts shows itself either as particles or as a wave. Here matter shows 'tendencies to exist'. As Capra explains it: 'In the formalism of quantum mechanism these tendencies are expressed as probabilities and are associated with quantities that take the form of waves; they are similar to the mathemetical forms used to describe, say, a vibrating guitar string, or sound wave.'[6]

In fact the picture of the atom, with its nucleus with electrons – as particles – circling around it, can now also be envisaged as a number of standing waves around the nucleus. The scientist Erwin Schrödinger sees each electron as a segment of vibrations (figure 5). In a similar way Guy Murchie makes a comparison between the vibration of the atom and that of a bell (figure 6).

A new development in physics seems to go even further in reducing the entire manifestation to vibrations. The fundamental building block of nature would consist of 'super-strings', minuscule vibrating strings, one hundred billion times smaller than a proton! All the different fundamental forces, all the particles in nature would be different vibrations of these super-strings![7] In this way we can see an endless variety of vibrations. They range from solid matter to light and radiation, to sound, and to thoughts and emotions. Inayat Khan sees matter as consisting of dense vibrations, while less material and invisible phenomena are finer vibrations. He describes the infinite range of different vibrations as follows:

> Vibrations as a rule have length as well as breadth; and they may last the least fraction of a moment or the greater part of the age of the universe. They make different forms, figures, and colours as they shoot forth, one vibration creating another; and thus myriads arise out of one. In this way there are circles

beneath circles and circles above circles, all of which form the universe.[8]

Spirit and matter

We then come to the question 'what is spirit' – as opposed to the material world – including its finest vibrations of sound and thought. Spirit and matter have always been considered as fundamentally different. Inayat Khan describes these opposites very clearly: 'Life has two divisions, of which one is accepted but the other is not yet. The accepted division of life is what we call substance; the division of life which is not yet accepted can be called vacuum.'[9]

Science has indeed discovered the enormous importance of this vacuum, this emptiness. What seemed to be concrete matter now appears, under further analysis, to consist of atoms in which very small electrons circle around a very small nucleus. These movements take place in a void, a vacuum that forms by far the largest part of the area within the atom. But what is this emptiness? We cannot observe anything of it even with the most refined instrument and therefore we consider this as 'nothing'. Inayat Khan, however, then makes the mystic's leap: 'But in reality vacuum is everything and all things'.[10]

The difficulty is that we cannot observe this vacuum with the same methods with which we observe even the most refined substances. But in reality this vacuum, which is all, is *spirit*. Inayat Khan again: 'That which goes beyond substance is spirit. Spirit is the absence of matter, even in its finest form.' Therefore it is in reality the all-pervading Divine Spirit, in which we live and move and have our being, as the Bible says.

Having in this way made a clear distinction between matter and spirit Inayat Khan then brings these two concepts together again, making this clear with a comparison:

'In the same way as ice and water are two things and still in their real nature are one, in the same way it is with spirit and matter. Water changes into ice during a certain time, and when the ice melts, then it changes again into water.'[11] And again: 'In reality matter comes from spirit; matter in its true nature is spirit; matter is an action of spirit which has materialized and has become intelligible for our senses of perception, and has thus become a reality to our senses, hiding the spirit under it.'[12] A little further on in the same book he gives the same picture, when he speaks about substance and vacuum: 'Substance has been composed in vacuum and has developed in it; it has formed itself, it has constructed itself and it will again be dissolved in the vacuum.'[13]

The process by which spirit becomes matter works through vibration. By vibration the spirit becomes first audible, then visible, and finally tangible. Here Inayat Khan quotes words from the Bible: 'In the beginning was the Word, and the Word was God'. He then describes this process: 'Vibrations turn to atoms and atoms generate what we call life; thus it happens that their grouping, by the power of nature's affinity, forms a living entity; and as the breath manifests through the form so the body becomes conscious.'[14]

This thought appears to be completely in line with the vision of modern science. F Capra has explained this clearly in his book *The Tao of Physics*.

> The relation between the virtual particles and the vacuum is an essentially dynamic relation; the vacuum is in reality a 'living Void', pulsating in endless rhythms of creation and destruction. The discovery of the dynamic quality of the vacuum is seen by many physicists as one of the most important findings of modern physics. From its role as an empty container of the physical phenomena, the void has emerged as a dynamic quantity of utmost importance. The results of modern physics thus seem to confirm the words of the Chinese sage Chang Tsai: 'When one

knows that the Great Void is full of Ch'i [vital energy] one realizes that there is no such thing as nothingness.'[15]

The question then remains: what is this spirit which becomes matter by vibration, and which, by this means, becomes first audible and then visible? Here Inayat Khan says that spirit cannot be defined in our concepts, but it could be seen as 'pure intelligence'. He does not mean intelligence in the sense of intellect, this concept goes beyond the knowing quality. Finally he comes to this formula: 'When consciousness is not conscious of anything it is pure intelligence. It is in this realization that the greatest secret of life can be revealed.'[16]

This spirit is working in and through the whole creation, in every being. The spirit working in man is the soul. Inayat Khan compares the soul to a ray of the divine sun. On the one hand, these rays show themselves separately, but on the other they are one, as the radiation of the one sun. This is also the case with souls.

In this way we can understand the fundamental unity of the whole of creation. This unity emerges also in a much more complex way in the vision of science. Thus David Bohm uses the concept of 'unbroken wholeness' and Capra describes the world vision of modern science as 'one indivisible, dynamic whole whose parts are essentially inter-related and can be understood only as patterns of a cosmic process.'[17] He expresses this also by pointing out that: 'As we penetrate into matter, nature does not show us any isolated basic building blocks, but rather appears as a complicated web of relations between the various parts of a unified whole.'[18] This becomes clear when we analyze the atom: 'The subatomic particles – and therefore, ultimately, all parts of the universe – cannot be understood as isolated entities but must be defined through their interrelations.'[19]

There is an inspiring parallel between this vision and

Inayat Khan's explanation of what he calls the 'threefold aspect of nature':

> The most interesting fact that emerges from the study of these three aspects is that they exist in every thing, in every being, and in every condition, and that without them nothing can exist. Only, if in studying these three aspects we continue to see them as three, then we have missed their secret; but if we learn to see them as one and the same, then we have profited by the observation of these three distinct aspects.[20]

He also describes examples of this threefold aspect of nature in human and religious terms. In human activity there are three aspects to loving: the lover, the beloved and love. There are also three aspects to knowing: the knower, the known and knowing (or the knowing faculty). In religion we have the Hindu *trimurti*: Brahma, the Creator; Vishnu, the Sustainer; and Shiva, the Destroyer or Assimilator. We also have the Christian Holy Trinity of the Father, the Son and the Holy Ghost.

But Inayat Khan sees this threefold aspect in all things and beings. And indeed in the atom we see the nucleus and the electrons kept together in a strong mutual relationship; the interrelationship which, as we saw, defines them. Molecules are also glued together in strong relationships. Murchie even speaks of 'the strong and basic, almost sexual, craving of abundant oxygen to unite with other elements.'[21] Thus we see similar principles or forces working in the endless variety of the universe. This brings us again to David Bohm's 'unbroken wholeness'. In Bohm's view: 'This enfolded order unfolds in the explicit order, the world that we see and in which everything is separated. And then he says, that this implicit order and the super implicit order beyond this suggests that there is a creative intelligence underlying all this.'[22] This corresponds to Inayat Khan's vision of the divine spirit expressing itself in all beings and in all aspects of the manifestation. When asked the question whether 'every atom of the manifestation can be said to have a soul', he replied:

> Certainly, because manifestation commenced from the heavenly source, from the divine spheres. Therefore every atom of this universe, mental or material, is an outcome of that source and cannot exist without having a part of that heavenly radiance within it. Even a mote of dust has a radiance behind it and if it were not for this radiance it would not have manifested to our view.
>
> We see it because it has light in it; it is its own light that shows it to us. That is its soul.
>
> What seems to be void of Intelligence is not in reality void of it, only the Intelligence is buried in its heart. It is, so to speak, Intelligence that has projected itself, and then its own outcome has covered it and buried the Intelligence in itself; but the Intelligence must come out some day. Therefore, through all these phases of life it is trying to break out. You can see this in volcanic eruptions. This power is working in floods, lightning, stars and planets. Its desire is to burst out when it is in a way captive, and its chance of rising is in human life. For that reason spirituality is the only object of fulfilment in human evolution.
>
> *Question*: Is that what is meant in the expression: the spiritual realization of matter?
>
> *Answer*: Yes.[23]

The creative process

When we begin to grasp this vision of the essential unity of creation, we can also begin to understand its origin. Modern science is developing fundamental speculations on point zero and the Big Bang and is constructing different theories about the origin of the universe. But here one begins to touch on mysteries which go beyond exact thought. In fact these theories raise matters that are profound and mysterious.

Inayat Khan has given us his mystic version of the creative process in the introduction to his masterful work, *The Soul, Whence and Whither*:

Before manifestation what existed? *Dhat*, the essence of Being, the truly Existing, the Only Being. In what form? In no form. As what? As nothing. The only definition that words can give is: as the Absolute. In Sufi terms this existence is called *Ahadiyyah*. A consciousness arose out of this Absolute, a consciousness of existence. There was nothing of which the Absolute could be conscious – only of its existence. This stage is called *Wahdah*.[24]

Wahdah also means consciousness of sound.[25] While *dhat*, the Absolute, is silent, unmoving, abstract life, in the first creative stage of *wahdah* the first vibration develops as sound. After that:

> Out of this consciousness of existence a sense developed; the sense – I exist. It was a development of the consciousness of existence. It is this development which formed the Ego, the Logos, which is termed *Wahdaniyyah* by the Sufis. With the feeling of I-ness, the innate power of the Absolute, so to speak, pulled itself together; in other words, it concentrated on one point. Thus the all-pervading radiance formed its centre, the centre which is the divine Spirit, or the *Nur*, in Sufi terminology – *Arwah*.[26]

This centre of radiation or *nur* can be compared to the sun. Inayat Khan explains this further:

> This Sun is that aspect of the Absolute God in which He begins to manifest and His first step towards manifestation is contraction, that contraction which is seen in all living beings and in all objects. It is first contraction that takes place and next expansion, which comes as a matter of course, as a reaction. The former tendency is the desire of inhalation and the latter exhalation. The contraction and expansion seen in all aspects of life comes from God Himself.
>
> The omnipresent Light by this tendency becomes concentrated and it is this concentrated Light of Intelligence which is the Sun recognized by the mystics. Shams e-Tabriz mentions this in his verse: 'When the sun of His countenance became manifest, the atoms of both worlds began to appear. As His light fell every atom donned a name and a form'.[27]

Thus this step in the creative process is characterized by spiritual light. The expansion of this light – following naturally after the contraction which is its origin – 'has been the cause of the whole of manifestion'.[28]

This process of manifestation has also been summarized by Inayat Khan:

> This centred light then divided existence into two forms: light and darkness. In point of fact there is no such thing as darkness, there has never been darkness. There is only more light compared with less light. This light and darkness formed *akasha*, or in Sufi terms *asman*, an accommodation, a mould; and the phenomenon of light and shade working through this mould furthered the manifestation into a great many accommodations, *asmans* or *akashas*, one within the other, and one over the other. Every step manifestation has taken has resulted in a variety of forms made by the different substances which are produced during the process of spirit turning into matter. The working of this process has been according to the law of vibration, which is the secret of motion. It is the plane of definite forms of nature which is called by the Sufis *ajsam*.
>
> Out of these forms came gradually from the mineral, the vegetable kingdom; from the vegetable, the animal kingdom and from the animal the human race, *insan*, thus providing for the divine Spirit – the bodies – *ajsam* – which it has needed from the time it centred itself on one point and from there spread its rays as various souls.[29]

> The manifestation is the exhalation of God, and what is called by Hindus pralaya – destruction or the end of the world – is absorption, which is the inhalation of God.[30]

This immense vision of Inayat Khan of the beginning and the end of the creation seems to show some similarity to that astronomical theory that assumes a 'Big Squeeze' before the presently expanding universe so that we could have

> a kind of pulsating or bouncing universe that would alternately expand and contract like a lung or a beating heart, as distinct

from the so-called hyperbolic universe that must expand without limit. The latter universe, according to the 'purest' mathematical requirement, must also have contracted (before the Big Squeeze) from 'an infinitely thin state an eternity ago', the two sides of the Squeeze holding a mysterious mirror symmetry to each other – an implosion–explosion, involution–evolution balance that can be compared with the approach and departure of a comet and may ultimately provide the key to an understanding of time.[31]

6

The Voyage of the Soul

In the previous chapter we were shown the grandiose nature of the creative process that Hazrat Inayat Khan has given us. We have seen that the spirit works in and through the whole of creation. In man this spirit is the soul, which is a ray of the divine sun. In his series of lectures on 'The Soul, Whence and Whither,'[1] Inayat Khan unfolds a magnificent vision of the culmination of the creative process in the experience of man's soul; during its voyage to the earthly plane, during its life on earth and in returning to the divine source. This vision is unique because of the clarity and authority with which he is able to explain, sometimes in amazing detail, the experience of the soul in the heavenly spheres – between God Himself and the earth. One feels that Inayat Khan knows about such matters, although to us they are mostly hidden behind the veil of death. How does he have such knowledge? Let him answer in his own words:

> The question: how does a prophet know of this? – may be answered by saying that the soul of the prophet is like a fruit which, because of its weight on the branch, touches the ground. It has not dropped on to the earth, it is still connected with the branch to which it is attached, the branch which comes through all the planes of existence. So he, in his experiences, so to speak, touches all the different worlds. It is this mystery which is hidden behind the prophetic genius and the prophetic inspira-

tion. It is through this current that the fruit is connected with the stem. Therefore, though on the earth, the prophet speaks of heaven; though on the earth, he calls aloud the name of God. While to many God is an imagination, to him God is a reality.[2]

He also says that 'every prophet has spoken to his followers in the way they could understand' about the other world. Thus, while the vivid pictures of heaven and hell given in earlier times were adapted to the understanding of those times, Inayat Khan's much more subtle explanation arises wholly from his own philosophical vision of the creative process, a vision which is in line with modern scientific thinking and is thus perfectly plausible to the modern mind.

The angelic spheres

The soul, as a ray of the divine sun, arrives first at the plane of existence which is close to that radiant source of divine being called the angelic heaven, and is then described as an 'angel'. Some souls remain in this plane; others, having a greater power, a stronger impulse of the divine spirit behind them, proceed onwards. As to the question of whether angels have a form, Inayat Khan says that this is 'very subtle and most difficult to explain in words'.

> The reason is that every thing or being that has a name, has a form, but we are accustomed only to call something which we can see a form, and what our eyes cannot see – we do not call it a form. To conceive the form of an angel, we must become an angel: we must turn into an angel to conceive what the true angelic form is. We are accustomed to picture every form like our own, therefore whenever we think of fairies or angels, spirits or ghosts, we picture them like us. The fairies of the Chinese have Chinese features and the fairies of the Russians have Russian hats, because the mind pictures what it is accustomed to see.[3]

In reality angels are beings of light (*nur*). They are vibrations. They are near to God. The angelic spheres are free from passions and emotions.[4] The souls living there are free from earthly distinctions and differences. The angels know only happiness, which is the true nature of the soul; their nature is to love and be ready to believe.

This mystical truth has been expressed in Christian imagery by depicting angels – sitting on clouds and playing on harps. The harp and its music are symbolic of the fact that angels are living vibrations. Showing them on clouds means that they are above the earth's temporary pleasures and pains.

> Such souls who are in direct touch with the Spirit of God and who have no knowledge of the false world which is full of illusion, who live and know not death, whose lives are happiness, whose food is divine light, make around the divine spirit, which is called *nur* by the Sufi, an aura which is called *arsh*, the highest heaven.[5]

These angels are inexpressibly happy, enjoying the light and life of God. Although generally they do not communicate with human life, yet some of them are destined to perform a certain duty on earth.[6] They can be messengers, bringing a warning or help to those souls on earth who are open to them, who have kept a link in their heart with the higher spheres. These are mankind's guardian angels. The angels are life-currents whose nature is to collect and to create. In the angelic heavens they collect atoms of radiance.[7]

Those souls which have the power to continue their journey to the earthly plane then meet souls who have returned to the angelic heavens again; they are tuned by them, by their feeling and rhythm. This turning then determines the line they will follow in their further voyage.[8]

The Sphere of the *jinn*

Having thus passed through the angelic heavens, these souls come to the sphere of the *jinn* or *genii*. 'This is the sphere of the mind and may be called the spiritual sphere, for it is mind and soul which make the spirit.'[9] Inayat Khan explains the *jinn* as follows:

> The *jinn* is an entity with a mind, but not such a mind as that of man, a purer, clearer mind, which is illuminated by the Light of Intelligence. The mind of the *jinn* is deeper in perception and in conception, because it is empty – not filled with thoughts and imaginations as is that of man. It is the mind of the *jinn* which may be called the empty cup – a cup into which knowledge can be poured, in which there is accommodation.[10]

The *jinn* sphere is a world of poetry, music, art, science and philosophy, of thought and imagination. The *jinn* gain their knowledge (their name is related to the Sanskrit word *jnana*, which means knowledge, and to the Latin *genius*, deity of generation and birth) by intuition and inspiration. It is a very free world, not limited as in the earthly sphere.

Life in the sphere of the *jinn* can be compared to the life of birds and deer in the woods, living freely in nature. Time in this world is incomparably different: life is much longer there. In this spirit sphere the soul builds its mind by attracting *jinn* atoms. This mind acts as a dress or vehicle which enables the soul to live in that world. The form of it is difficult to comprehend by us, accustomed as we are to physical forms, which do not belong to the sphere of the *jinn*.

Jinn are able to contact souls on our earth and they are able to help one another. In one way it is easy for a *jinn* to aid a human being, because he has such a freedom of movement. But it can also be quite difficult, because a human being can be so absorbed in earthly thoughts and actions as to be resistant to influences from the *jinn* sphere.

Those *jinn* that have the power and desire to travel still further will then meet with returning souls from whom they can learn much. The *jinn* receive a 'map of the journey toward manifestation', as Inayat Khan puts it.[11] They receive the impressions of the mind of one, or a few, returning souls by a process of reflection, a phenomenon that plays an important role through the whole manifestation. In this way the *jinn* mind receives the impression of the personality of the returning soul, while the latter does not lose anything. The empty cup of the mind of the *jinn* soul can then be filled so completely with these impressions that the *jinn becomes* that with which he is impressed. In this way the personality of the returning soul can come back to the earthly plane. This is Inayat Khan's explanation of the true meaning of reincarnation. It is the personality – with which men tend to identify – which reincarnates; the soul, as a divine ray, is attracted back to its origin.

Arrival on the physical plane

Continuing its journey towards manifestation, the soul then reaches the physical plane. The soul being born has been pictured as Cupid, an angel which shoots its arrows into the hearts of a man and a woman, bringing them together in love. Philosophically this can be explained as: 'Duality in every aspect of life and on whatever plane is creative, and its issue is the purpose, the outcome, of the dual aspect of nature.'[12]

In this way the loving couple 'opens the way for this new coming soul to enter physical existence'.[13] The new-born baby immediately cries. Why? Inayat Khan says because it finds itself in captivity, in a strange new place.

The body which the soul receives as its instrument – or vehicle – to live on earth is, as Inayat Khan puts it so beautifully, 'an offering from the whole universe'.[14]

It is not offered to the soul only by the parents, but by the ancestors, by the nation and race into which the soul is born, and by the whole human race. This body is not only an offering by the human race, but is an outcome of something that the whole world has produced for ages: a clay which has been kneaded a thousand times over; a clay which has been prepared so that in its every development it has become more intelligent, more radiant and more living; a clay which appeared first in the mineral kingdom, which developed in the vegetable kingdom, which then appeared as the animal kingdom, and which was finished in the making of that body which is offered to the new coming human soul.[15]

Hoyack describes this process as two lines of evolution – one vertical, the other horizontal – that meet each other in the birth of man. The vertical line is the soul, the spirit travelling from the light of the angel sphere to the denseness of the earth; an *involution* of the finest vibrations of the spirit into the denser vibration of matter. The horizontal line is the physical *evolution* from mineral to man as it is analyzed by science. In this way man, in whom the two lines meet, is the culmination of the process of manifestation.[16] When observing this process 'one feels like saying that not only man, but the whole manifestation was created in the image of God'.[17]

So the soul, born on earth, contains three beings: the angel, the *jinn* and the human. According to the depth of the impressions received in the different planes he or she shows the qualities of the angel and of the *jinn*. The impressions received from returning souls in the *jinn* sphere give the individual specific qualities and tendencies. In addition he or she receives the heritage of his or her earthly ancestors. Inayat Khan describes this also as the soul 'borrowing' properties from the *jinn* and from the physical world. At the same time the soul takes up the obligations and responsibilities attached to these properties.[18]

During this earthly life the soul desires to collect earthly properties. In fact, this is what induces the soul to come on earth; it is the desire to approach near it, to take possession of it, to utilize it to its best advantage, and to guard against its being taken away. This is the nature of the soul. This is the difference between the socialistic point of view and the mystical idea. The socialist says: 'That is unjust', and he does not see that it is nature and natural. Without this, life would not have been possible.[19]

The body that the soul has received in this way has been constructed as a perfect instrument to experience life to the full. That which is perceptible, it makes clear. For this purpose we have the five senses, through which we can taste, smell, touch, hear and see.

Thus 'the body may be likened to a glass house made of mirrors'.[20] This is clear for the eye, but the nature of the other senses is the same.

> The eye stands as a mirror before all that is visible, it reflects all that it sees. The ears are the accommodation for the re-echo of every sound that falls upon them. In other words, they are the mirror of every sound. The senses of touch and of taste are grosser compared to the senses of sight and hearing; at the same time their nature is the same. All the different sweet, sour and salt savours, and the feeling of warmth and cold are perceived by them, and they stand as mirrors in which taste and touch are reflected.
>
> Therefore, as one sees oneself reflected in the mirror, so this body stands as a mirror in which every experience of the outer life is reflected and made clear. If the mirror is dusty, it does not reflect the image clearly; so the experience of life is not clear, when the body is not looked after according to the spiritual point of view.
>
> The Sufis say that the body is the temple of God, but the right interpretation of this saying would be that the body is made to be the temple of God.[21]

It follows from this that care of the body is important. Inayat Khan even calls it 'the first and most important principle of religion'.[22]

Besides the outer senses there are also the centres of inner perception. These are the intuitive faculties, an accommodation where the thoughts and feelings of another can be perceived – the atmosphere of a person or place; and if these senses are keen, even past and future can be perceived.

Due to our artificial and materialistic life, however, these centres are often blocked. This causes depression and confusion, because the inner longing to see is not quite satisfied. Though these centres are located in the body, they are of a much finer matter that can only be nourished by the finer energy which we attract through the breath and through the vibration of sound and words. This therefore plays an important role in Sufi training.[23] (See chapter 10)

The two most important inner centres are those of the heart and the head. Sufi training develops both these centres together, which brings about balance.

When a human receives his or her body, his or her mind is completed. Before birth on earth it was only an accommodation (*akasha*), as Inayat Khan describes it, an accommodation moulded by the impressions that have fallen on the soul during its voyage to the earthly plane. This *akasha* becomes the mind when it has been connected with the body.[24]

The character of the mind

Inayat Khan describes the character of the mind as a mirror.[25] We have already seen that it is by reflection that the soul, in the jinn world, receives the impressions of the personality of a returning spirit. In our earthly life the soul also reflects all the impressions which it receives. These come through the senses: all that we see, hear, smell, taste or touch impresses us. In that way all our different experiences in our relations with other people as well as our own actions create strong impressions. We are also impressed by thoughts and feelings, by the spoken or written word; or, as indicated earlier, by direct perception through the inner centres. All these impressions are reflected in the sense that they fill and characterize the mind as long as it is focussed on these impressions. But as a mirror the mind can turn easily to other impressions, thoughts and feelings and be filled with those. In *The Mind World*[25] Inayat Khan discusses how this phenomenon of reflection plays a role in the whole manifestation; also in the animal world (where, for example, a horse will reflect man's willpower and obey him) and even in plants which – as recent research has shown – react to different kinds of music and to the way in which they are cared for.

The impressions which one receives are projected again to others, to the surroundings. In this respect the mind also resembles the mirror. But the mind is more than just a passive mirror: it has a memory and it is also creative.

Its memory means that impressions once received are registered and remain preserved after the mind has turned away from them for the time being and is busy with other things. These impressions can then be re-lived, re-thought and re-experienced at a later date. The more this is done the stronger and deeper will the recording line of these impressions become. In this way the mind collects learning and experience and develops a certain way of acting and behaving – its character. Thus the individual seems to be what his or her mind contains; in a certain way these impressions *are* the person.

The mind is also creative. It works with its impressions. It can think about them, deepen its feeling about them in the heart. They can be expressed in words and they can motivate us to certain actions. Through the mechanism of reflection other people then react to these thoughts, words and actions. The radiating effect of our thoughts and feelings can be so strong and pervasive that certain happenings and events in our life can be attracted by them in a way which we are unable consciously to understand. In this way our whole life is determined by those thoughts and feelings which have a dominant influence in our mind. Determined, we could say, by the direction in which the mirror of our mind is often positioned; or by our attitude in life. Very often this mechanism brings about a more or less automatic development in our life in which certain deeply felt experiences and impressions in our life carry us further in a direction which we do not really desire. Thus, for example, a failure which has impressed us strongly can create a continuing fear of failure which will attract further failures.

But we need not and should not allow our life to take a course – influenced by outside events – which does not correspond to our inner wishes. For behind the mind is the soul, a divine ray – as we have seen – an emanation of the divine creative spirit. In that spirit is a hidden power which can direct the mind and our life in the desired way. We can do this when we become conscious of this power which is our divine heritage, when we open our mind to it. We have to realize then that we are responsible to the divine spirit – not only for our actions, but also for our thoughts and feelings. The key to developing this mastery of life – directed from the soul – is to choose consciously to which impressions we give our attention – which will feed and strengthen them – and which undesirable impressions we do not allow to influence us. It is the art of 'seeing and not seeing, hearing and not hearing' – refusing to give further attention to impressions that we find undesirable.

In this way we can develop the strength to reach our objectives in life. The question then arises what these objectives should be. What is the purpose of our life? In his book, *The Purpose of Life*, Inayat Khan says that 'the first step on the spiritual path is when a soul realizes its outer purpose in life'.[26] He also quotes Saa'di: 'Every soul is created for a certain purpose and the light of that purpose has been kindled in that soul.'[27]

The path of attainment

If one seeks one will find this purpose, and trying to attain this purpose gives meaning to our life. In the beginning it may be a limited and material purpose, nevertheless striving for it is 'a step on the spiritual path'. By working towards it we learn, we make progress and this will enable us, when our first purpose has been realized, to aim for a higher ideal. Thus Inayat Khan says that 'in the end all purposes resolve into one purpose and it is that purpose which is sought by the mystic'.[28] He then discusses how we are able to progress to the final mystical purpose through five aspects: our desire to live, our desire to know, our desire for power, our desire for happiness and our desire for peace. These are the fundamental and all-embracing desires which are behind most earthly purposes. Inayat Khan offers us practical psychological recommendations as to the manner in which we can be successful and reach our objectives, overcoming the many difficulties on our way. This teaching on 'the path of attainment' is very important for our outer life. In briefly summarizing these teachings, which have not yet been published in their fullness, I can say the following: one needs in the first place to develop *concentration* – keeping one's attention, one's thoughts and feelings directed to the purpose. One should keep *confidence* that the purpose will be attained in spite of all the difficulties. One's *reason* must be used to find ways to solve these difficulties successively. So progress should be gradual; it is dangerous to want to reach the objectives too quickly, as that could exhaust one's strength and be counter-productive. Inayat Khan has said that there are many in this world who, with their enthusiasm, kick away the object of their attainment like a football. One must first have made oneself ready to attain the purpose; have acquired the needed power for it. Therefore one needs *patience* – learning to wait for the right time to make a certain step forward. Patience is difficult, but it builds inner strength.

All this means that from beginning to end *self-discipline* is needed: keeping one's eye on the object; not giving in to anger and emotion easily; not allowing oneself to be tempted by deviations; all this requires self-discipline. This also means that certain sacrifices have to be made in order to accomplish our purpose. Additionally, self-discipline is needed to maintain silence about our plans as much as possible. By silence one preserves the energy which is necessary to accomplish our object; one also prevents criticism and opposition. When we persevere in this spirit our goals will be reached. Inayat Khan is very positive about this. He points to the divine power of the soul which can attract all that one really desires. The Almighty God will answer the longing of the soul. As Christ said: 'Ask, and it shall be given you; seek, and ye shall find; knock, and it shall be opened unto you.'[29]

Progressing along this path of attainment we can aim step by step for higher ideals. The five fundamental desires mentioned earlier can then finally lead us to the ultimate inner realization. Finding physical life limited in time, we can discover the eternal life of the soul; beyond the limits of earthly knowledge we can discover the knowledge of the divine being; we can come in touch with the Almighty Power of God; and we can find the real happiness of the soul, beyond all disturbing influences of life.

What happens in this ultimate realization of the soul's longing is that it becomes conscious of itself, of its own divine being, united with God and illuminated by God. The soul, which is a ray of the divine light – or divine intelligence, that has been caught by its instruments of mind and body – has been completely occupied by its interests in the experiences which it receives through these instruments. But at some time it will find these experiences disappointing and then it turns around and directs its attention to itself. Inayat Khan has described this process:

As in order to make the eyes see themselves one has to take a mirror to see the reflection of these eyes, so in order to make this real being manifest, the whole being, the body and mind, have been made as a mirror, that in this mirror this real being may see itself and realize its independent being. What we have to achieve by the path of initiation, by the way of meditation, by spiritual knowledge, is to realize it by making ourselves a perfect mirror.[30]

In chapter 8, on mysticism, we will pursue the important subjects of initiation and meditation, which are the essence of the Sufi path. The object of this path is God-consciousness, which can be attained by self-realization. In this self-realization the purpose of the manifestation is realized. Inayat Khan has answered the question of the purpose of the manifestation:

It may be answered in one word: satisfaction, for the satisfaction of God. Why is God not satisfied without it? Because God is the Only Being, and the nature of being is to become conscious of being. This consciousness experiences life through various channels, names and forms; in man this consciousness of being reaches its culmination. Plainly speaking, through man God experiences life at its highest perfection.[31]

Life after death: the soul's return to God

After the experience of earthly life, death comes for every one. This can be when the soul has fulfilled its purpose on earth, 'when its flower has come to its full bloom', so that there is nothing more to hold the soul. But it can also be when

for some reason or other, either by disorder or by having been worn out, this body loses that power of keeping together by which it holds the soul which functions in it. It gives way, and the soul naturally departs, leaving the material body as one would throw away a coat which one no longer needs.[32]

Then the objects and desires of the soul may not yet have been fulfilled. But now life goes on in the other spheres – first in the *jinn* world. Death is an illusion, caused by man's attachment, his identification with his body, which in reality is only a cover, a dress over mind and soul. In reality death is only a transition to the other life.

As he has described the voyage of the soul toward the earth, so Inayat Khan has also described many aspects of the continuing life of the soul in the higher spheres. As we have seen, he does this through his mystical inner connection with the heavenly spheres which gives him a direct perception of these worlds. And it is striking that the indications he gives about the afterlife correspond in many respects with recently recorded near-death experiences.[33] Many people who have recovered from a serious illness or accident in which they were considered clinically dead, report how they left their body and saw it, for example, lying on the operating table, while they heard the doctors speaking together. There followed a brief experience of beginning to live in another world of which they could describe a number of aspects.

Such descriptions, by very different people, are strikingly similar. In a few cases, however, people did not remember anything after their near-death.[34]

This may correspond with Inayat Khan's explanation that the soul of a person who dies convinced that there will be nothing after death will be paralyzed for some time and be in a state of inertia by this very idea. This state may be called 'purgatory'. But after this there comes a new impulse of life which enables the soul to begin to experience life in the *jinn* sphere. Souls who have not had this idea that death finishes everything move into the new world immediately. Inayat Khan describes this world:

> And what does the soul see in this bright daylight? It sees itself living as before, having the same name and form, yet progressing. The soul finds a greater freedom in this sphere and less limitation than it had previously experienced in its life on the earth. Before the soul now is a world, a world not strange to it but the world which it had made during its life on the earth. That which the soul had known as mind, that very mind is now

to the soul a world. That which the soul, while on earth, called imagination, is now before it a reality. If this world is artistic, it is the art produced by the soul. If there is an absence of beauty, that is also caused by the neglect of beauty by the soul while on earth.[35]

After death the soul continues its voyage with the mind. The contents of the mind – all the experiences registered in its memory – determine the life of the soul on the *jinn* plane; this is the real meaning of heaven and hell. When our life on earth has been happy, and we have made other people happy, then we take this happiness with us to the other world. When we have been unhappy, causing harm to other people, we take that poison with us. At first, therefore, we continue with the same thoughts and feelings and the same kind of 'work' as on earth.[36] 'But it is not bound to the same work, for the reason that it is not subject to the same limitations as it was while on earth. The soul eventually rises to that standard which was the standard of its ideal; it does that work which was its desire.'[37] This other world gives a much greater freedom and has fewer limitations. The soul has a greater power therefore in this world to accomplish its objects and desires.

In this world the soul also has a mental or spirit body. What does this body look like?

It looks exactly the same as one was on the earth. Why must it be so? Because of man's love for his body. Does it change? Yes, if he wishes it to change. If the soul wishes it to be changed, it can be changed according to its own ideal.[38]

There is also a language of the sphere of the *jinn*, which is more indistinct and yet more expressive than our language.

These spirits (returning souls with a mind) can still see the conditions on the earthly plane very clearly – if they wish to.[39] They are able to communicate with souls on earth; but these souls cannot hear them clearly. For 'there is a wall which only stands before those who are still on the earth, but not before the ones who have passed over to the other side.'[40] But people on earth can sometimes receive the communication of the spirit unconsciously; and carry out their wishes, thinking they are doing this of their own free will.[41]

Moody's record of near-death experiences corresponds to this. He discusses what can be looked upon as 'the absence of limitations' in this world, which he explains as follows: 'Think of it this way: A person in the spiritual body is in a privileged position in relation to the other persons around him. He can see and hear them, but they can't see or hear him.'[42] He also describes the spiritual body:

> Furthermore, despite its lack of perceptibility to people in physical bodies, all who have experienced it are in agreement that the spiritual body is nonetheless something, impossible to describe though it may be. It is agreed that the spiritual body has a form or shape (sometimes a globular or an amorphous cloud, but also sometimes essentially the same shape as the physical body) and even parts (projections or surfaces analogous to arms, legs, a head, etc.). Even when its shape is reported as being generally roundish in configuration, it is often said to have ends, a definite top and bottom, and even the 'parts' just mentioned.[43]

The idea in some sacred scriptures that there would be a Judgement Day after death, when recording angels summed up all the soul's good and bad deeds, really means that when the cover of the body has been taken away from the soul, the mind will be very clear, so that the soul can immediately oversee its whole life on earth. As Inayat Khan says: 'The recording and the judgement are in reality in the heart.'[44]

This is confirmed by Moody when he states that 'it is interesting to note that the judgement in the cases I studied came not from the being of light, who seemed to love and accept these people anyway, but rather from within the individual being judged.'[45] The mind becomes clear in the afterlife, because the soul heals its instrument in going over to the other world:

> Freeing itself from all the impressions of illness, of sadness, of
> misery which the soul has experienced while on earth and has
> taken into the spirit world, it heals its own being, and renews
> the tissues of that body which still remains with it after it has
> left the physical body. It purifies itself from all illness and the
> impression of illness, and thus renews the life in the spirit world
> in accordance with its grade of evolution.[46]

The soul then lives a long time in the sphere of the *jinn*. Time
is very different there from here, on the earthly plane. Everything lasts much longer.[47] It is during this time that the soul
encounters other souls on their way to the earth. By a process
of reflection, comparable to the developing image on a pho-
tographic plate, they impart their experiences on earth, their
qualities, convictions and attitudes, to these souls who are
coming to earth. These souls then also take over 'guarantees,
contracts, mortgages and all the accounts that the spirit had
left unfinished on the earth – these they undertake to pay or
to receive when coming on the earth'.[48] And the returning
souls do not lose anything in this process of reflection; this
exchange makes the giver richer still.[49] When this giving is
done consciously 'there is great joy for that spirit'.[50] This
relationship is like that of a child to his parent or a pupil to his
teacher.[51] Meanwhile the returning soul constantly busies
itself in the *jinn* world to accomplish its objectives.

> There are objectives which remain unfulfilled in one's lifetime
> on earth. They are accomplished in the further journey in the
> spirit world, for nothing that the human heart has once desired
> remains unfulfilled. If it is not fulfilled here, it is accomplished
> in the hereafter. The desire of the human soul is the wish of God,
> small or great, right or wrong, and it has a moment of fulfilment.
> If that moment does not come while the soul is on the earth
> plane, it comes in its further journey, in the spirit world.[52]

What a positive and inspiring vision Inayat Khan gives
here! Whatever our problems and disappointments in the
earthly life, at the end, in the afterlife, all desires will be

fulfilled and all problems solved. For:

> The source of the soul is perfect, and so is its goal. Therefore, even through its limitation, the soul has a spark of perfection. The nature of perfection is no want. The limitation that the soul experiences is on the earth, where it lives the life of limitation. Still, its one desire is perfection, to achieve and obtain all it wants. So this want is supplied for the very reason that the Perfect One, even in the world of variety, does everything possible to experience perfection.[53]

In its divine perfection the soul is also invulnerable to all the bad experiences of earthly life. These will create impressions in the mind, but the soul itself remains pure and will in the end purify the mind and then detach itself from it to reunite with the Divine Being.

On its journey to this destination the soul leaves the *jinn* sphere and moves on to the heaven of the angels. This transition is also a kind of death, a death coming after a much longer time, 'a death that is not so severe as on the earthly plane, where everything is crude and coarse; but a change is slightly felt after a very long time of the fulfilment of every desire.'[54]

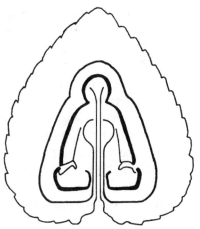

Figure 7 Soul, mind and body

The angelic heavens

The soul now leaves its garb of the *jinn* world behind. It leaves all thoughts behind but takes with it its feelings, the feelings that it has collected. Its life is in vibrations, it is a sound, a tone (Sanskrit *sura*). The body of the soul is changed very much in entering the angelic heavens. It becomes a *luminous being*, a body of radiance and light. Light here is life; it is audible, visible and intelligible.[55] The size of this body of the angel is larger than the body of the *jinn*, as that body is larger again than the physical body. Yet these bodies of *jinn* and angel also enter into the innermost being of man (see figure 7).

The occupation of the angels is to be around the Light and Life of God, as bees around a flower.

> Divine beauty it sees, divine air it breathes, in the sphere of freedom it dwells, and the presence of God it enjoys. Life in the heaven of the angels is one single music, one continual music. Therefore it is that the wise of all ages have called music celestial, a divine art. The reason is that the heaven of the angels is all music.[56]

Thus the happiness of the angels is incomparably greater even than the joy of the *jinn* sphere and their life is longer again than that of the *jinn*. But their only aspiration is to get closer to the Light.

In the angelic heavens – as we have seen – there are also meetings between souls departing from the source and those returning to it. For the returning souls the time finally comes 'when the soul is most willing to depart even from that plane of love, harmony and beauty, in order to embrace the source and goal of love, harmony and beauty which has attracted it through all the planes.'[57] Then the soul throws off its radiant garment and reaches its destination in God.

> The soul, drawn by the magnetic power of the divine Spirit, falls into it with a joy inexpressible in words, as a loving heart lays

itself down in the arms of its beloved. The increasing of this joy is so great that nothing the soul has ever experienced in its life has made it so unconscious of the self as this joy does. But this unconsciousness of the self becomes in reality the true Self-consciousness.[58]

Even so, there is an important difference between this way of becoming unconscious of the self and coming to this realization consciously.

The difference is like that between a person having been pulled back with his back turned to the source, and another person having journeyed towards the goal enjoying at every step each experience he has met with, and rejoicing at every moment of this journey in approaching nearer to the goal.

What does the soul, conscious of its progress towards the goal, realize? It realizes at every veil it has thrown off a better life, a greater power, an increased inspiration, until – having passed through the spheres of the *jinn* and the heavens of the angels – it arrives at a stage when it realizes that error which it had known and yet not fully known, the error it made in identifying itself with its reflection, with its shadow, falling on these different planes; as if the sun, forgetting at that moment that the sunflower was only its footprint, had thought on looking at it, 'I am the sunflower'.[59]

7

Our Relation to God: the God-ideal

Images of God

What is the relationship between ourselves and God, the divine source of the soul, the creator of the universe?

In the depth of our being we naturally long to become conscious of this relationship. But this is difficult, as we are completely caught and surrounded by this material world, obsessed by our outer senses. We would like to see and feel God. It is therefore understandable that the earliest worship was of the sun, the sun that rose each day and nourished us with its warmth; the sun that was far away, beyond reach yet all-important for the life of the universe. Indeed, as we have seen, the comparison of God creating souls with the sun and its rays, can help us to understand the mystery of the creative process.

But as we developed our scientific knowledge of the universe and discovered the nature of the sun, the earth and the other planets, this image of God was destroyed. We began to realize that God is invisible and inaudible to our outer senses. Yet we feel an inner urge to search for Him. To develop our relationship to God we then needed another, an unearthly image of God. It is difficult for us to understand and imagine God in our mind. For (as Hazrat Inayat Khan says in the *Gayan*): 'All things existing have their opposite, except God; it is for this reason that God cannot be made intelligible.'[1]

This is why from time to time prophets, divine messengers, have come to humanity to indicate a way to God; to give inspiring and evocative images and ideas of God's being. They realised God; they were still in contact with the divine spirit and source; and they were inspired to evoke the mystery of God's being in human language.

Many aspects of God that have been suggested to us in this way are the opposites of the various limitations of man. Thus *Saum*, the first prayer in the Universal Worship of the Sufi movement, starts in this way: 'Praise be to Thee, Most Supreme God, omnipotent, omnipresent, all-pervading, the only being . . .' As man's power is always limited, so God is omnipotent. As man can only be in one place at a time, God is omnipresent and all-pervading. In this way, we read in one of the oldest sacred scriptures, the *Bhagavadgita*:

> You are all we know, supreme, beyond man's measure,
> This world's sure-set plinth and refuge never shaken, Guardian
>   of eternal law, life's Soul undying.
> Birthless, deathless; yours the strength titanic, Million-armed,
>   the sun and moon your eyeballs,
> Fiery-faced, you blast the world to ashes,
>
> Fill the sky's four corners, span the chasm
> Sundering heaven from earth. Superb and awful is your Form
>   that makes the three world tremble.[2]

Here also we find many aspects contrary to man's limitations:

> 'a refuge never shaken' – while an earthly refuge is always
>   fragile
> 'guardian of eternal law' – while our laws always change and
>   pass
> 'life's soul undying, birthless, deathless' – while we are mortal,
>   are born and die.'

Also very poetic is this passage from the *Bhagavadgita*, surely with some memory of sun-worship: 'Suppose a thousand suns should rise together into the sky: such is the glory of Infinite God'.[3] And in the Qur'an, the latest of the sacred scriptures, we read:

> In the name of God, Most Gracious, Most Merciful.
> 1. Say: He is God, The One and Only;
> 2. God, the Eternal, Absolute;
> 3. He begetteth not,
>   Nor is He begotten;
> 4. And there is none
>   Like unto Him.[4]

While all such aspects are uplifting because they picture God's being as beyond all our human limitations and weaknesses, they may also suggest a great distance between God and ourselves. They are more abstract.

Of all religions, Buddhism is the most abstract because of its devotion to the truth. But that truth, which is eternal, which brings happiness and peace, longs to become conscious. The following Buddhist text makes this clear:

> The things of the world and its inhabitants are subject to change; they are products of things that existed before; all living creatures are what their past actions made them; for the law of cause and effect is uniform and without exceptions.
>
> But in the changing things truth lies hidden.
>
> Truth makes things real. Truth is the permanent in change.
>
> And truth desires to appear; truth longs to become conscious; truth strives to know itself. There is truth in the stone, for the stone is here; and no power in the world, no God, no man, no demon, can destroy its existence. But the stone has no consciousness.
>
> There is truth in the plant and its life can expand; the plant grows and blossoms and bears fruit. Its beauty is marvellous, but it has no consciousness.
>
> There is truth in the animal; it moves about and perceives its surroundings; it distinguishes and learns to choose. There is

consciousness, but it is not yet the consciousness of Truth. It is a consciousness of self only.

The consciousness of self dims the eyes of the mind and hides the truth. It is the origin of error, it is the source of illusion, it is the germ of sin.

Self begets selfishness. There is no evil but what flows from self. There is no wrong but what is done by the assertion of self.

There is misery in the world of Samsara; there is much misery and pain. But greater than all the misery is the bliss of truth. Truth gives peace to the yearning mind; it conquers error, it quenches the flames of desire and leads to Nirvana.[5]

Here we find the same vision of the evolution of the manifestation that we have described earlier as emanating from the divine spirit. Clearly, in the words of Inayat Khan: 'God is truth and truth is God'.

But to answer the need for a personal relationship to God more personal images of God have also been given. This is very clear in the Jewish scriptures which give a special relationship between God and Israel and urge man to love God, to fear Him and to serve Him. The following text is a good example:

And now, Israel, what doth the Lord thy God require of thee, but to fear the Lord thy God, to walk in all his ways, and to love him, and to serve the Lord thy God with all thy heart and with all thy soul,

To keep the commandments of the Lord, and his statutes, which I command thee this day for thy good?
. . .
For the Lord your God *is* God of gods, and Lord of lords, a great God, a mighty and a terrible, which regardeth not persons, nor taketh reward;

He doth execute the judgement of the fatherless and widow, and loveth the stranger, in giving him food and raiment.

Love ye therefore the stranger; for ye were strangers in the land of Egypt.

Thou shalt fear the Lord thy God; him shalt thou serve, and to him shalt thou cleave, and swear by his name.[6]

And in the New Testament, the Christian Scriptures, God is often described as the Father in heaven, the Judge and Forgiver of our shortcomings, the Creator.

Thus there are many aspects and images of God. At first sight they appear to differ between different religions and this has often led to misunderstanding, to conflict, even to religious wars. But when we study the sacred scriptures more deeply, we find that the same holy book often gives both abstract and more personal pictures. Thus the *Bhagavadgita* combines the abstract passage, quoted above, with a very moving personal plea:

> Take our salutations, Lord, from every quarter,
> Infinite of might and boundless in your glory,
> You are all that is, since everywhere we find you.
>
> Carelessly I called you 'Krishna' and 'my comrade',
> Took undying God for friend and fellow-mortal,
> Overbold with love, unconscious of your greatness.
>
> Often I would jest, familiar, as we feasted
> Midst the throng, or walked, or lay at rest together;
> Did my words offend? Forgive me, Lord Eternal.
>
> Author of this world, the unmoved and the moving,
> You alone are fit for worship, you the highest.
> Where in the three worlds shall any find your equal?
>
> Therefore I bow down, prostrate and ask for pardon;
> Now forgive me, God, as friend forgives his comrade,
> Father forgives son, and man his dearest lover.[7]

On the other hand the New Testament, besides personal images, also gives the very mystical text where Paul found the altar to the unknown god in Athens, a text which culminates in the inspiring words: 'In Him we live and move and have our being'.

The evolving God-ideal

Thus we can see that we need not question which images are right and which are wrong. In a sense they all have their shortcomings, since they are expressed in human words and concepts and appeal to our minds. The reality of God is beyond our minds. It remains a mystery to our thinking. Still, we need a picture or pictures of different aspects of God to be able to develop our relationship to God. For this reason Hazrat Inayat Khan has introduced the concept of the 'God-ideal': the ideal picture of God that everyone with some belief has to make for him- or herself. It is the most uplifting and inspiring picture that one can imagine on the basis of one's own understanding of the creation. This God-ideal is not the reality of God; it is a human imagining; as such it is different for different individuals; and it will evolve over time for each of us as our understanding grows. Inayat Khan sees the evolving God-ideal as a ladder along which we can climb upwards step by step, closer to God. Then we can begin to establish a relationship to God that becomes more and more real in our life as it awakens an echo – in the depth of our being, in our soul, beyond the limitations of our mind. This is our first task in the inner life. Inayat Khan makes this clear:

> The first and principal thing in the inner life is to establish a relationship with God, making God the object with which we relate ourselves, such as the Creator, the sustainer, forgiver, judge, friend, father, mother and beloved. In every relationship we must place God before us and become conscious of that relationship so that it will no more remain an imagination . . . [8]

He continues in the next passage: 'The work of the inner life is to make God a reality, so that He is no more an imagination; that this relationship that man has with God may seem to him more real than any other relationship in this world . . .'[9] This has always been the Sufi ideal. But how can we follow this path in the present time?

In our own scientific age many people have great difficulty in this because they feel that the traditional way of seeing God is indeed just an imaginative concept but has no reality. The traditional picture of God sitting in heaven on a throne clearly cannot fit into a more scientific view of creation.

So how may we, being aware of the scientific view of the world, build a God-ideal which is in harmony with scientific understanding? We have already seen that this scientific view of the world is in harmony with the idea of an omnipresent life force or energy, a more abstract picture, which corresponds to the mystical saying in the New Testament: 'in Him we live and move and have our being'. But such an abstract picture does not appeal to our feelings; it is difficult to experience a personal relationship with it. One of the most important and illuminating aspects of the Sufi message is that Inayat Khan builds a bridge between a scientific and philosophical view of reality and the more personal God-ideal that we need.

For Inayat Khan, who has described the abstract, mystical God-ideal more clearly than anybody, states in *The Unity of Religious Ideals* that it is of great importance for us to start our religious development with a personal ideal. He says that people who have read many books and who have thought about the soul and the spirit – as we have done in the previous chapter – 'have eaten of the Truth without digesting it'.[10] What does this mean? 'Digesting' means completely assimilating truth into our being, so that the idea becomes part of us and obtains a real meaning in our life. That does not happen just by having an interesting abstract concept. For the inner life it is important that we develop a living relationship so that we have the feeling that we can surrender to God, that we can humble ourselves before Him, that we can forget our limitations. That gives a completely different experience. Inayat Khan recommends us 'to begin by worshipping the personal God', and then 'we should allow our soul to unfold in the abstract God' . . . 'The realization of the abstract God is the satisfaction which comes after we have perfected the worship of a personal God.'[11]

But in this scientific age we are still left with the question: how to build a bridge between that abstract concept that we know is the truth, and a God-ideal that enables us to develop the living relationship to God that we need? To link together the abstract vision and the personal God-ideal, Inayat Khan says in *The Unity of Religious Ideals*: 'If God has no personality, how can a human being have a personality – we human beings who come out of His own Being, we who can express the divine in the perfection of our souls?'[12] He then makes the comparison that 'if the bubble is water, certainly the sea is water'. How can the bubble be water and not the sea? He compares the human soul to a drop and God to the ocean. The drop is small compared to the enormous ocean, infinitesimally small, and yet it is of the same material: 'If we are the drop and we are a personality, then God, the ocean, must also be a personality.' He works this out in the following passage:

> If it is the very same spirit which we breathe from space that makes man an intelligent being capable of thinking and feeling, the same spirit that gives him the power of perception and conception and develops in him that feeling which one calls 'ego', 'I'; if this is the phenomenon that the spirit shows by being absorbed by the material body,[13] how much more capable of perception and conception, of thought and feeling must be the spirit in itself. Only, because we are limited by our physical frame we are not able to experience fully its perfect life and its perfect personality.[14]

Man's relationship to God

This is certainly a very inspiring bridge between the two approaches.

In this way we get a wonderful picture of God: on the one hand the all-pervading, only being in which we all move; on the other hand we can still see this all-pervading being as a perfect personality, with a perfect mind, all-powerful and guiding the whole creation including our individual life. The wonderful thing that is so important to realize is that as drops of water are to the ocean so are we all related to God. There is indeed a very personal relationship between us and God; this is not imagination, it is very real and it governs our life; but often we keep our eyes closed to it. We are caught in the intoxication of our life, acting and being absorbed in it; but if we open our eyes and observe life, looking at what it has to tell to us, then we can find the divine guidance coming to us in many different forms. We can see it in a most subtle way, we can find it in our own heart, in our intuition. To be able to feel this, we must be able to still our mind; then we can hear the voice of God directly. But if we are not sufficiently able to do this, it can come to us from outside, in a sign in nature, in some happening with a symbolical meaning, in a dream. Inayat Khan teaches us that even if we do not listen to all this, we can receive warnings from a friend, or if we still don't listen, a warning from an enemy (which is less pleasant). And if we still go on with closed eyes, we will finally have an experience in life that teaches us. The consequences of our actions come to us. Thus, in life we can constantly learn. It is important to recognize this, to see that God can guide us in our life. To illustrate this relationship Inayat Khan makes a comparison with the mother and the child. The child wishes to run away independently, to explore life; the mother lets it go, but still keeps an eye on it, she wants it to experience a little bit but not too much. But when the child comes to the mother and wishes to be guided and takes her hand, then it is guided much more closely. In the same way, if a man looks for divine guidance, then God gives special guidance.

In this way we can develop that personal relationship that is so important for the inner life. Then we can begin to make it a reality; we can gradually begin to feel that this relationship which we feel in the depths of our being is indeed the most important relationship to us. This creates a miracle in our life, it makes us strong and independent. Nobody can take this away from us. It can help us in all conditions of life; it can help us to overcome limitations. In surrendering to God we will be filled with the power of God. Thus we can understand the paradox which the mystic shows to us: the greatest humility and at the same time the one who lives the inner life can become more powerful and more loving because he will see that same spirit in all men. The flow of love that develops in our hearts is the most powerful force that can bring us closer to experiencing and touching the divine. In that way we can fulfil the meaning of our life.

Unity of religious ideals

The idea of the God-ideal enables us to understand the fundamental unity of religious ideals as it is taught in Universal Sufism. As the God-ideal must have somewhat different aspects, a different flavour, so to speak, for different individuals, to uplift them from their own way of thinking to the divine sphere, so it will also show differences in different cultures during different historical periods. The words in which the religious ideal is expressed have to correspond to the culture of the times. But with all their outer discrepancies the different religions all lead man in the direction of the One and Only Being. Hazrat Inayat Khan makes us understand how from time to time a divine messenger has come when humanity loses its way, when the God-ideal is no longer alive, but becomes buried under rigid dogmas which no longer inspire mankind. These messengers appear as human beings, in a form that appeals to the people of their time; and they explain the eternal truth in a way which inspires the most. What radiates from them, their vibration, is able to pierce through the outer thinking of humanity and awaken our consciousness to the divine being.

In this way the sacred scriptures which have been left to us – although often written down some time after these divine messengers had left the earthly plane – can continue to inspire us.

At the present time, when transport and communication facilities have brought different religions so much closer together, it is very necessary that their essential unity should be more widely understood. There is one God; so religion, teaching man to serve God and to pray to God, ought to bring humanity together in one brotherhood/sisterhood. To spread and to illustrate this mystical concept of the essential unity of all religions Hazrat Inayat Khan established the Universal Worship as the religious activity of the Sufi movement. This is a form of worship in which a ritual symbolizes how the same divine light is brought to humanity through different religions. This is done by lighting candles for each of the various religions from the one light which represents the light of God.

A passage is then read from the different sacred scriptures on the subject that is discussed in the sermon. This Universal Worship is performed not by professional priests but by members of the Sufi Movement who receive a special ordination, while continuing their work in the world. Men and women participate equally in this service. Thus all religions speak with their own voice in the Universal Worship. We can be inspired by all of them; and followers of different religions can join together in this Universal Worship, finding something from their own religion and unity with others, opening their mind to an inspiring word from other religions. This Universal Worship is now performed in many Sufi centres around the world.

Its purpose is to bring the different religions together, not to create a new religion. It gives a symbolical expression to a mystical understanding. When Inayat Khan speaks about 'the coming world religion' he means something beyond ceremony, dogmas or even God-ideals. It would be 'something living in the soul, in the mind and in the heart of man'.

And what is it? The Hindus have called it *dharma*, which in the ordinary meaning of the word is duty. But it is something much greater than what we regard as duty in our everyday life. It is life itself. When a person is thoughtful and considerate, when he feels his obligations towards his fellow-man, towards his friend, towards his father or mother, or in whatever relation he may stand to others, it is something living, it is like water which gives the sense of living to the soul . . .

This is the religion which has been the religion of the past and will be the religion of the future. All religion taught by Christ or any other of the great ones, was intended to awaken in man that sense which is awakened when religion is living. It does not matter then into which building one goes to pray, for every moment of one's life has become religion – not a religion in which one believes, but a religion which one lives.

What is the message of Sufism? Sufism is the message of digging out that water-like life which has been buried by the impressions of this material life.

That living thing in the heart is love. It may come forth as kindness, as friendship, as sympathy, as tolerance, as forgiveness, but in whatever form this living water rises from the heart, it proves the heart to be a divine spring.

And when once this spring is open and is rising, then everything that a man does in action, in word, or in feeling is all religion; that man becomes truly religious.

If there is any new religion to come, it will be this religion, the religion of the heart.[15]

8

Mysticism: Unity with God

The mystical experience

In the previous chapter we have seen how we can develop our relationship to God by building the God-ideal that is most uplifting for us. This ideal evolves with our understanding and spiritual growth. Thus the ideal serves as a ladder, enabling us to climb closer to God, making our ideal more and more beautiful, higher and higher so that it approaches perfection. In this way we can develop a living relationship to God, praying to Him, feeling and accepting God's guidance in our life. Gradually we can then reach the stage where we recognize the divine in all beings, where we accept all life's experiences as coming from God. Through our love for God, we see the divine spirit working in the whole creation. Thus we may develop a saintly spirit.

It is the longing of the mystic to go even beyond this: to climb further in order to really experience God, to come in contact with the divine reality behind all images. While in the religious relationship man and God are still felt as separate, the mystic aims at unity with God, forgetting his limited being in order to become immersed in God's consciousness. The false self is transcended, the true self is discovered. Inayat Khan has described this mystical stage:

In this stage the Sufi hears through the ears of God, sees through the eyes of God, works with the hands of God, walks with the feet of God; then his thought is the thought of God and his feeling is the feeling of God. For him there is no longer that difference which a worshipper makes between himself and God; as Khusrau the Persian poet says, 'When I have become Thee and Thou hast become me, when I have become body and Thou hast become soul, then, Beloved, there is no difference between I and Thou'.[1]

In fact, the mystic having first sought God everywhere externally finally finds God internally, in his or her own soul. This is expressed poetically in the *Gayan*:

> I searched, but I could not find Thee; I called Thee aloud, standing on the minaret; I rang the temple bell with the rising and setting of the sun; I bathed in the Ganges in vain; I came back from Ka'ba disappointed; I looked for Thee on the earth; I searched for Thee in heaven, my Beloved, but at last I have found Thee hidden as a pearl in the shell of my heart.[2]

What happens in the mystical experience can be described, in the abstract, as turning the mirror of the mind around: from the outer world on which it has mostly been focussed, to the inner world, so we can become conscious of the divinity of our soul and thus of God. Inayat Khan explains:

> The soul has two different sides and two different experiences. One side is the experience with the mind and body, the other side is the experience of the spirit. The former is called the outer experience, the latter the inner experience. The nature of the soul is like glass, transparent; and when one side of the glass is covered it becomes a mirror. So the soul becomes a mirror in which the outer experiences are reflected when the other side is covered.
>
> That is why, however greatly blessed a person may be with outer knowledge, he is not necessarily gifted with inner knowledge. In order to attain to inner knowledge the Sufi covers the other side of the soul, so that its mirror part may face the spirit instead of the outer world. As soon as he is able to accomplish this he receives inspirations and revelations.[3]

This has also been expressed in a different way: that the individual must become as an empty cup so that he or she can be filled with divine light and inspiration. Such a mystical experience is indescribable in words; it is beyond thought and feelings. It is the experience of the soul itself: that of pure consciousness. It is completely fulfilling, it is an ecstasy in which one can still remain sober. It is the essence of all knowledge.

> There remains no part of one's being that is hungry. There is a feeling of everlasting satisfaction in knowing something that the knower can never put into words. It is this knowledge that mystics call self-realization, and that is recognized by some religious-minded people as God consciousness, and by philosophical minds as cosmic consciousness.[4]

As the experience of unity with the essence, with the spirit of the whole creation, mysticism is basically the same in all religions. It is the unifying core in all religions. Ways and methods to approach this experience may differ, but the ultimate experience is one; and this unity radiates through all inner religious experience.

An important difference in method is related to the outer life. Hindu and Buddhist mystics in the East have often withdrawn from life in the world, living in nature and following ascetic methods. They have focussed completely on the inner life. The way which Inayat Khan recommends for the present time is a human way. The Sufi aims for balance between the inner and outer life. Life in the world is considered a positive opportunity to gain experience that the soul has been longing for and as a challenge to fulfil the purpose of our life, to meet our obligations and to develop sympathy for our fellows. Widening our consciousness in this way also opens the way for our inner life. It helps to overcome our personal limitations with which we tend to identify ourselves, so that this blocks our inner progress. On the other hand the inner life is a source of inspiration for our outer life. Balancing our inner and outer life brings us to the fullness of life.

Thus, the Sufi approach to mysticism has two aspects:

1. *spiritual training*: learning to become conscious of the inner life;
2. *mental purification*, with respect to our attitude in the outer life.

Spiritual training

The aim of spiritual training is to become conscious of the soul, our deepest being. This is difficult, because our attention is continuously drawn to the outer life, where we are active with our mind and body. From the beginning of life on earth we see ourselves as a separate being, different from all others. We have our own name, by which everyone recognizes us. We are born in a certain place, from certain parents; and this determines our start in life, and our first experiences. These experiences form deep impressions in our mind which give a certain direction to our thinking and feeling and certain ways in which we react to what happens to us. This forms our character. As life continues we learn and have more experiences which add to the contents of our mind and often deepen our earlier thoughts and feelings. Thus we develop our own mind-world with problems, desires and purposes which keep us constantly busy in the outer life. In fact we are so intensely occupied with all this that we identify ourselves with this limited being of mind and body. We are not conscious of more than that, we have quite forgotten our real being, our soul. Inayat Khan has compared our situation with that of a traveller: we look from the window of our train or car at constantly changing, fascinating landscapes, and we are so absorbed in this that we forget ourselves. This is the intoxicating illusion of the outer life. We have to begin to see through this, to detach ourselves from it in order to discover the real life, the life of our soul. That is the aim of mysticism. But this is not something that is meant only for specially gifted mystical personalities. For everyone there comes a time sooner or later when one becomes dissatisfied with the intoxication of the outer life. When one has gained certain experiences and achieved certain aims in outer life one finds that the satisfaction of all this diminishes. A longing arises for a deeper, more fulfilling happiness and more peaceful experiences. Inayat Khan calls this 'the awakening of the soul'. We begin to realize that just as we are not our body, but that our body is an instrument for us to use, so it is with the mind. With all its thoughts and feelings, its memories, its reason and its ego it is also an instrument that we use. But what are 'we' then? To begin to discover that, we must be ready to turn away from all this activity of mind and body. We have to make our body and mind quite still. Sitting still, in a suitable posture, we must let our thoughts and feelings come to rest, let them disappear from our consciousness; not by trying to force them out, but by becoming indifferent to them. To the extent to which we can do this, we will discover an inner experience, quite unconnected with anything in our outer life. This experience cannot be adequately described. It is subtle and light, both in the sense of uplifting and of inner illumination; and it is very peaceful. When one is first touched by this one feels that it can become much more intense and delightful.

But it is very difficult to attain this restful silence. As soon as we sit with closed eyes and try to be still, all kinds of thoughts and feelings arise and keep our mind busy. We find that we lack control of our mind, which is like a restless and undisciplined horse. That is why spiritual training is needed. What we must first learn in this training is to become the master of our mind. For that purpose the mystical schools have used practices of *concentration* and *contemplation*.

Concentration is, of course, of vital importance to both inner and outer life. We would not be able to achieve anything if we could not focus our attention and our energy on it during the necessary time. The more we concentrate on a certain activity – forgetting everything else – the more efficient and creative will we be in that activity. When we are interested in a certain activity this concentration can develop in a very natural way. It is the secret of all success.

The conscious concentration that is practised in spiritual training is more difficult, because its purpose is to make the mind still. For that purpose we have to keep the mind completely focussed for some time on a single object, picture or symbol. This will prepare the mind to become still.

A development of this is contemplation, where we focus our mind on one thought, one idea. This is a subtler and more abstract practice; it goes deeper. In the Sufi schools the subject of such contemplation is always related to God, the source and centre of all inner light and life, with which we need to reconnect ourselves. By contemplating certain divine qualities and aspects we are not only training our mind, we are also deepening our relationship to God. The reflection of that divine quality in our mind will become creative so that we can develop such a quality in our own life and personality. In this way such practices of contemplation can help us also to guide our life in the direction of our deeper inner longing. But the highest of these contemplative practices in Sufism goes beyond particular qualities. Here the idea is that this whole manifestation is a world of illusion that has no independent existence; that in reality God alone exists. This means also that our mind and body are only instruments for the divine spirit to become conscious of itself. Our body is a temple of God.

In the Sufi tradition these contemplative practices are done with the help of continuing repetition of sacred words which express the idea of the divine quality on which one is contemplating. Such sacred words are often taken from Arabic as the Indian mantras are taken from Sanskrit, both older languages whose words preserve an original sound which expresses their meaning; they therefore impress us more deeply. Their sound, their vibration immediately touches our heart.[5] The sacred words used in the Sufi training have an additional power, because they have been used for centuries by Sufi mystics. They bring one subconsciously in contact with the living magnetism of that word and sound in the collective consciousness of humanity.

Such words have to be given as a wholly personal prescription by an authorized initiator, a spiritual guide on the path; the *mureed* (the disciple) must consider them as a sacred and secret trust. For this reason this important aspect of Sufi mysticism cannot be explained here in further detail.

Breathing practices are also an essential element in spiritual training. All mystics have recognized the importance of breath, of the right way of breathing, of controlling the breath. Inayat Khan has given us many beautiful and impressive explanations of this mysterious subject.

> Breath is the very life in beings, and what holds all the particles of the body together is the power of the breath, and when this power becomes less then the will loses its control over the body. As the power of the sun holds all the planets so the power of the breath holds every organ. Besides this the breath purifies the body by taking in new and fresh life and by giving out all gases that should be put out. It nourishes the body by absorbing from the space the spirit and substance that are necessary, and more necessary than all that man eats and drinks.[6]

This leads to the spiritual meaning:

> Breath is a channel through which all the expression of the innermost life can be given. Breath is an electric current that runs between the everlasting life and the mortal frame. Those who have attained any intuition or miraculous power or any power have achieved it by the help of the breath. But the first

essential thing is a pure channel for the breath, and that channel is the human body. If the channel is blocked, there is no possibility for the breath to flow freely. Air in itself is not bad, but when it touches the earth, it partakes the influence of the earth, and therefore can become polluted. So it is with the breath; breath in itself is pure, but if the channel through which it works is not right, it becomes impure.[7]

Therefore, in order to make spiritual progress, it is necessary to purify the channels of the breath and to make the breath finer. For this purpose breathing practices are given, which can become a powerful help on the path to God. 'Breath, to a Sufi, is a bridge between himself and God; it is a rope for him, hanging down to earth, attached to the heavens. The Sufi climbs up by the help of this rope.'[8] And the breath can then also be used as an instrument to help keep the mind focussed in concentration and contemplation.

> Mystics therefore find a rope to tie the mind in a certain place where it cannot move. What is that rope? That rope is breath. It is by that rope that they bind the mind and make it stand where they wish it to stand. It is like the bird which uses its saliva to make its nest; so is it with the mystic who out of breath creates atmosphere, creates light and magnetism in which to live.[9]

All these practices are only a preparation for what a seeker in the spiritual path is longing for: *meditation* and *realization*. In the practices described so far one is active, using one's willpower to purify and to still body and mind. This, says Inayat Khan, is 'the boundary of human progress, and further than that is divine progress'. At the boundary one has to become passive, opening oneself, surrendering in silence to the divine spirit. This stage of meditation, which can then come to one, is best described in Inayat Khan's phrase of 'mystical relaxation'. Relaxation comes naturally after a physical or mental exertion of willpower. In this way, after the exertion of concentration and contemplation, when our body and mind have become still, we can relax naturally. In this silence, without thoughts or feelings, we can experience the pure consciousness; the divine spirit can touch us.

> The third stage is meditation. This stage has nothing to do with the mind. This is the experience of the consciousness. Meditation is diving deep within oneself, and soaring upwards into the higher spheres, expanding wider than the universe. It is in this experience that one attains the bliss of meditation.[10]

> The third part of concentration is meditation. In this grade one becomes communicative; one communicates with the silent life, and naturally a communication opens up with the outer life also.[11]

Through these experiences the seeker can finally come to the stage of realization.

> Realization is the result of the three other grades. In the third kind of experience man pursued meditation; but in this, meditation pursues man. In other words, it is no longer the singer who sings the song, but the song sings the singer. This fourth grade is a kind of expansion of consciousness; it is the unfoldment of the soul; it is diving deep within oneself; it is communicating with each atom of life existing in the whole world; it is realizing the real 'I' in which is the fulfilment of life's purpose.[12]

Mental purification

In this way spiritual training enables us to open the door to inner knowledge, to raise our consciousness above the denseness of the earth. It is a vertical line of progress. When we are living in the world, we have to complement this inner path, where meditation raises us above the mind world, with a process of purifying the mind. For as long as our mind remains tied by rigid and limited thoughts and ideas, and while our heart is poisoned by antagonistic feelings towards others, we can try to turn away from all this for a short time, but such an impure mind will soon re-attract the soul's attention. The soul will be caught again in the unhappy prison of the mind. Events in the outer life will cause confusion and disturbances, keeping a grip on our consciousness.

Real spiritual progress therefore requires a certain attitude in our outer life that can lead to mental purification. There we follow a horizontal line of progress, described by Inayat Khan as an 'expansion of consciousness'.

A first aspect is called 'unlearning'. We start our life by learning, from our parents, at school and in university, the many things that we need in life. We continue to learn from our experience and we build our character, our customs and certain beliefs and convictions. All this limits our mind and tends to make it rigid.

When we wish to come to the inner life, we have in a sense to reserve this process by unlearning. At first sight this seems a puzzling concept. What is meant by it?

> Spiritual attainment, from beginning to end, is unlearning what one has learnt. But how does one unlearn? What one has learnt is in oneself. One can do it by becoming wiser. The more wise one becomes, the more one is able to contradict one's own ideas. The less wisdom one has, the more one holds to one's own ideas. In the wisest person there is willingness to submit to others. And the most foolish person is always ready to stand firm to support his own ideas. The reason is that the wise person can easily give up his thought; the foolish holds on to it. That is why he does not become wise because he sticks to his own ideas; that is why he does not progress.[13]

So one must begin to see and accept the relativity of one's thoughts and ideas. One must become more open to new ideas. An important and very practical guideline on this path is to learn to understand the point of view of other people. Inayat Khan has said: 'The Sufi sees everything from two points of view: his own and that of the other'. This goes against the tendency of most people to cling forcefully and often fearfully to their own point of view and to defend it passionately against other ideas. In this way one imprisons oneself within the limits of one's own thoughts and experiences. By seeing also from another point of view one widens one's outlook and opens one's mind to other and often enriching insights. One unties the 'knots' in one's mind.

In the beginning it may seem difficult to follow this guideline, but it often proves to be surprisingly practical. Working in the world we need to cooperate with other people and to do this successfully one needs to understand them. Bringing together different points of view, seeking a consensus, will often lead to a balanced approach that is well thought out. Even with those who oppose us, having different aims and interests, it works better when we try to understand their point of view. We might discover something of value that we can use ourselves. And it will help us to build bridges over differences, opening the way to cooperation or at least to a reasonable compromise.

In the history of science we can see how revolutionary new insights have been gained by opening one's mind to a new and very different way of looking at a certain problem.

A further aspect of mental purification is to be able to see the right of the wrong and the wrong of the right. We can rise above the rather limited measures of right and wrong that are in general use. This will also widen our horizon and give us a deeper understanding.

> Mental purification means that impressions such as good and bad, wrong and right, gain and loss, and pleasure and pain, these opposites which block the mind, must be cleared out by seeing the opposite of these things. Then one can see the enemy in the friend and the friend in the enemy. When one can recognize poison in nectar and nectar in the poison, that is the time when death and life become one too. Opposites no more remain opposites before one.[14]

In this way we learn to rise above the opposites out of which this earthly manifestation has been built. Beyond these opposites is the unity of God which pervades everything. It is this unity which the mystic is seeking. Mental purification opens the way to it.

These aspects of mental purification lead us to the deeper experience of purifying the heart. The heart is the depth of the mind, where we develop our feelings. When we begin to understand the point of view of our fellow man or woman and when the blocking element of rigid judgements of good and bad has been softened or taken away, we will begin to sympathize with others. We do not only understand, we can then feel with them – their feelings can be reflected in our heart and, quite naturally, a loving impulse of friendship, forgiveness, kindness and help will arise. This is a wonderful and liberating experience. It brings to our consciousness the underlying unity behind all different creatures and personalities. This gives a moral exaltation. As Inayat Khan says: 'Exaltation is a purifying process. A moment's exaltation can purify the evil of many years, because it is like bathing in the Ganges, as Hindus say.'[15]

It is by this purification of our thinking and feeling that we must – so to speak – clean the dust and rust of life from the mirror of our mind. If we then focus the mind on God, it can become the perfect mirror of God's being. This means ultimately that God becomes conscious of Himself by seeing His reflection in the mirror of our mind. This is the purpose of our life and even the purpose of the whole creation. This is where the cross, combining the vertical line of spiritual training and the horizontal line of expansion of consciousness, leads us.

Initiation and discipleship

Of course, it is not easy to follow this path. A whole life, focussed more and more on this ideal, may be needed for it, and it is very important to receive some guidance on this path.

Embarking on this inner voyage brings us to new and un-known territory, different from what we have learnt in our outer life. It is a privilege and a practical help therefore if one can be guided by someone who has already made some progress on this inner journey. To receive and follow this guidance, discipleship is needed. This has always played an important role in mystical orders of all religious traditions. Following a spiritual guide – a *guru* or *murshid* – was practised as an essential element. The relationship between teacher and disciple, between *murshid* and *mureed*, *guru* and *chela*, creates a deep spiritual link of mutual interaction and trust, of devo-tion and sympathy. It begins with initiation, by which the entry to the path is opened. The initiate receives the blessing of the teacher and promises faithfully to follow his guidance. The teacher then gives spiritual training by prescribing prac-tices which are suitable for the character and possibilities of the disciple. This is valuable as the correct choice and combi-nation of practices can play an important role. It is the expe-rience and inspiration of the teacher which enables him to make this choice, while the devotion and trust of the disciple in the teacher gives these practices a deeper meaning.

At the same time the teacher offers help in mental purifi-cation. He will open the eyes of the disciple to other views, other aspects of life. This will help the disciple in the difficult process of *un*learning. Deep trust in the teacher is needed for this, so that the disciple is ready to accept teachings which may differ from some of his own preconceived ideas. But the essence of this spiritual teaching goes beyond explanations in words. It is the finer vibration of the teacher, his radiance, which the disciple can receive in silence. This is a reflection of the higher consciousness of the teacher on the mind of the disciple, which enables him to discover the depth of his own being. The real teacher attunes his disciple, harmonizing his rhythm and feelings and in this way allows him in due course to discover the solution of his questions and problems himself.

In the Sufi movement, Hazrat Inayat Khan has created the Sufi Order – defined as its Esoteric School of Inner Culture – as its core activity. Those who are serious in their desire to follow the inner path can receive initiation and spiritual guidance within this Sufi Order. For those in the West, this is a unique opening into the wonderfully enriching and fulfilling world of mysticism where they can join the age-old caravan of the seekers of truth.

9

Moral Culture

Meaning of good and bad

As we have seen in chapter 8, in striving for mental purification the mystic should learn to see the right of the wrong and the wrong of the right. The mystic aims to rise above these opposites, which characterize the earthly manifestation. They are important for life in the world, where, as responsible human beings, we have to choose between right and wrong. But the mystic seeks God and God transcends these opposites. As Inayat Khan says in the *Vadan*: 'God cannot be good and perfect at the same time; it takes good and bad both to make perfection'. Realizing this, we can also understand philosophically how the all-powerful God guides his creation to a certain purpose by using all opposing forces.

> Naturally one then begins to see the law working in nature; one begins to see that the whole universe is a mechanism working towards a certain purpose. Therefore the right one and the wrong one, the good and the bad, are all bringing about one desired result, by wrong power and by right power, a result meant to be, which is the purpose of life.[1]

This also means that good and bad may be relative. What is good cannot always be determined objectively for all men

Hazarat Inayat Khan (1882–1927)

Sufi discipleship

Dargah (grave) of Nizam-ud-Din Aulia

Above left: Portrait of Maulabakhsh, Inayat Khan's grandfather
Above right: Inayat Khan's mother

Inayat Khan's
birthplace in Baroda

Inayat Khan as a young man

Inayat Khan in later life

Inayat Khan in the garden at Suresnes

Courtyard in front of Inayat Khan's *dargah* in New Delhi

Inayat Khan's *dargah*

Interior of
Qaytbay
mosque

The Sufi temple Universal Murad Hassil, Katwijk

and circumstances. 'As the people of different races, nations and religions each have their own standards of right and wrong, their own conception of good and evil, and their own ideas about sin and virtue, it is difficult to discern the law governing these opposites.'[2]

The question then arises: what is this law? What guidelines can we find for our moral conduct in practical life, while the mystical experience transcending good and bad has not yet been attained? Inayat Khan answers this question about the underlying law of good and bad in a way closely related to the mystical aspect of expansion of consciousness. Continuing the same passage he says:

> It becomes clear, however, when one understands the law of vibrations. Every thing and every being seem separate from one another on the surface of existence, but beneath the surface on every plane they are nearer to each other, while on the innermost plane they all become one. Thus every disturbance to the peace of the smallest part of existence on the surface, affects the whole inwardly. Therefore any thought, speech, or action that disturbs peace is wrong, evil, and a sin; but if it brings about peace it is right, good, and a virtue. Life being like a dome, its nature is also dome-like. Disturbance of the slightest part of life disturbs the whole and returns as a curse upon the person who caused it; any peace produced on the surface comforts the whole, and thence returns as peace to the producer. This is the philosophy underlying the idea of the reward of good deeds and the punishment of bad deeds given by the higher powers.[3]

A first important element in this passage is 'the law of vibrations'. This points to our feelings, to our rhythm. What are the feelings behind our actions; and what is the rhythm in which we act? This determines whether and how far these actions make others and ourselves happy. In that sense Inayat Khan also says 'verily all that leads to happiness is good'.[4]

The secret of this happiness – the real inner happiness – is related to the underlying unity of the creation. Peace makes us conscious of this underlying unity which is the essence of our being. Therefore 'any thought, speech or action that disturbs peace is wrong, evil and a sin; but if it brings about peace it is right, good and a virtue'.

We can experience peace in our heart when we open ourselves to the divine spirit. And we can practise it in our outer life by creating and maintaining harmony.

Harmony is a relationship between different tones, colours or beings with their feelings and thoughts, which creates beauty and awakens love. In that way the barriers between different beings are broken down and unity is experienced. Harmony is therefore an essential moral and spiritual ideal. This means that evil 'is something which is devoid of harmony, which lacks beauty and love, and above all it is something which does not fit into the accommodation of life'.[5]

Moral evolution

But how can we follow such an ideal in our daily life, which is always so full of conflicts and differences? In his book *Moral Culture* Inayat Khan provides a number of very practical and down-to-earth recommendations for our behaviour. The title is typical of his approach, which is one of evolution, of inner growth, not of rigid prescriptions. It is a gradual step-by-step development of widening our outlook and understanding and of overcoming our narrow egocentric tendencies. Instead of immediately being confronted with the highest moral ideal, we can start to follow this teaching at a level where for most of us our learning starts, in our simple daily life. We have many different kinds of relationships: with friends and enemies, with acquaintances and relations, with masters and servants – and with God. At this stage, we feel quite separate from all these other beings, we are sensitive to what they do to us and we are often prone to antagonistic feelings. At this stage we should aim to follow what Inayat Khan calls the law of reciprocity. 'This moral is natural to the one who sees the difference between himself and another, who recognizes every man as such and such.'[6] This law leads to balance, fairness and justice in our dealings with others. Thus it is a first approach to harmony.

The ideal of reciprocity may seem relatively easy; but we have to realize that our ego always tends to cause a certain asymmetry in our judgements. As Inayat Khan remarks with keen psychological insight: 'The self is always dearer to everyone, and when weighing our dealings with others we naturally give them more weight, and do not give the dealings of others with us the same weight.'[7]

To attain real reciprocity, this asymmetry has to be overcome:

> Therefore, in order to make a balance, we must always consider that a kind action, a good thought, a little help, some respect shown to us by another, are more than if we did the same to our friend; but an insult, a harm done to us, a disappointment caused to us by a friend, a broken promise, deceit, or anything we do not like on the part of a friend, should be taken as less blameworthy than if we did the same.[8]

Understood in this way, reciprocity becomes a first and important step in our moral development. And in his beautiful explanation of the meaning of this law of reciprocity in our different relationships, Inayat Khan always leads us to look beyond our limiting ego-concept. Thus, he urges us in general terms that:

> In dealing with another we ought first to consider in what relation we stand to him, and then to consider what manner of dealing would please us on the part of another who is related to us in the same way as we are to him. In all favourable actions we ought to do more than we should expect another to do for us; and in unfavourable actions we ought to do less than what we should expect on the part of another.[9]

In this way we can gradually expand our sympathy from those next to us to those further away and observe our duties to them. But we are warned that: 'A sense of generosity and willingness should go hand in hand with duty; if not, instead of a blessing it becomes a curse.'[10] This makes it clear yet again that our feelings, the motives behind our action, are more important than the action itself. Sincerity and sympathy give value to what we do for others.

All this is, of course, a concrete application of the expansion of consciousness which was described in chapter 8 as the horizontal complement to the vertical line of mystical upliftment. But reciprocity must also be applied in our relations with enemies. On this Inayat Khan is very realistic when he tells us that 'paying back insult for insult and harm for harm is the only thing that balances.'[11] At the same time we are recommended to be very careful: 'Our dealings with our enemy should be considered with more delicacy than our dealings with a friend.'[12] Thus the law of an eye for an eye should not be applied 'as long as there is a chance of meeting the enemy's revenge by kindness.'

And in general Inayat Khan advises us that:

> Precautions must be taken that nobody should become our enemy; and special care must be taken to keep a friend from turning into an enemy. It is right by every means to forgive the enemy and to forget his enmity if he earnestly wishes it; and to take the first step in establishing friendship, instead of withdrawing from it and still holding in the mind the poison of the past, which is as bad as retaining an old disease in the system.[13]

This clearly demonstrates the aspect of mental purification, which we have seen in the previous chapter; as an essential aspect of inner life and mysticism. In this way – and similarly in our other relationships – the correctly balanced reciprocity leads us to begin to understand others better by placing ourselves in their position, by looking at things from their point of view. Thus we can overcome exaggerated or imagined antagonisms in others and develop forgiveness and sympathy. This will lead us to the second stage in moral evolution: the law of beneficence,

> where man, recognizing himself as an entity separate from others and recognizing others as distinct entities themselves, yet sees a cord of connection running through himself and all, and finds himself as a dome in which rises an echo of good and evil; and in order to have a good echo he gives good for good and good for evil.[14]

Here, having begun to understand others and becoming conscious of how our relationships with them function, we begin to see how our thoughts and feelings are reflected in the minds of other people. And in the 'palace of mirrors' of the mind world, sooner or later, their echo returns to us. Then our concern will to radiate only loving and friendly feelings, so that these vibrations will come back to us in the dome of the universe. This consciousness of the cord of connection running through all seemingly separate beings leads·to Inayat Khan's psychological advice – which pervades the whole Sufi message – always to focus our mind on the good side of things, situations and people. This is neither blindness nor lack of insight; but it means that we choose consciously to which impressions we give attention so that they can deepen and grow in our mind.

It is the attitude of seeing and not seeing, leading to a certain knowing innocence.[15] Through this attitude we can become master of our feelings and thoughts and in this way master of our life. For in our experiences life gives us back what we create and radiate through our mind.

All this implies a very practical rule: to avoid judging and criticizing other people. We are always strongly tempted to do this; our mind likes to analyze others from our own point of view; and then we can feel that we are better. But in reality, by focussing our mind on weaknesses and shortcomings in others, we tend to create or encourage these weaknesses in ourselves, and our relationship with the person whom we criticize will be adversely affected by this. Untactful criticism can antagonize the other person and will often make him or her defensive and will therefore strengthen his or her faults. Even if we express our criticisms in his or her absence to a third person, it will influence our relationship negatively.

Inayat Khan uses this approach to explain the meaning of Christ's saying: 'Resist not evil'.

> Evil may be likened to fire. The nature of fire is to destroy everything that lies in its path, but although the power of evil is as great as the power of fire, yet evil is also as weak as fire. For as fire does not endure, so evil does not last. As fire destroys itself, so evil is its own destruction. Why is it said, do not resist evil? Because resistance gives life to evil; non-resistance lets it burn itself out.[16]

This means that we should not react in the same manner, with anger to anger. Although a natural reaction, this implies that one allows oneself to be infected with the same mood, the same evil so that it is allowed to spread and receives more nourishment. A chain reaction may then be the result.

By avoiding this, by controlling one's reaction, one can stand like a rock in the sea. One need not agree to the thoughts or wishes of the other; but by not allowing oneself to be influenced in one's own heart by negative feelings, one is much more likely to find a harmonious solution or compromise through inner strength and understanding.

Harmony should, however, always be seen in a sufficiently wide context: not only with the person with whom we are in immediate contact, but also in relation to others who are involved, in relation to a wider community and to our ideals.

Overcoming the false ego

It will be clear that it is not at all easy to apply these moral guidelines in practice. It requires a constant battle with our ego. The tenth Sufi thought puts it in this way: 'There is one Path, the annihilation of the false ego in the real, which raises the mortal to immortality and in which resides all perfection.'

This raises the fundamental question: what is the false and what is the real ego? Inayat Khan explains that the ego is as essential a part of our mind as thought, reasoning, memory and willpower. It originates when the soul, during its voyage, acquires the instrument of the mind and of the body. 'Our mind and body, being reflected upon a portion of the all-pervading consciousness, make that part of consciousness an individual soul, which in reality is a universal spirit.'[17]

We live from this consciousness; all that we experience through these instruments of mind and body is reflected upon our consciousness, our soul. These reflections of and through our mind and body then become so strong and fascinating in the beginning of our life on earth, that our consciousness is completely captured by them. In consequence, we tend to identify ourselves with our mind and body. We think that we *are* our mind and body.

This is the fundamental illusion of life, and the cause of all tragedies in life. This identification forms the false ego, and it is this illusion that has to be overcome, so that we can rediscover the true nature of our consciousness, our real ego which in reality is connected with the universal spirit.

All the difficulties which we experience on the path of moral evolution and expansion of consciousness are caused by this false ego. This ego constantly clashes with other egos, with conflicting interests, desires, thoughts and feelings. Thus our false ego is continuously challenged and irritated by these other egos. This disturbs harmony and peace in our heart; the more we fight for our interests and ideas against others, the more painful such disharmony will become. We can only create harmony by controlling, by training our ego. On this path Inayat Khan distinguishes three aspects of the ego:

the physical ego,
the mental ego and
the spiritual ego.

The physical ego develops as we become attached, even enslaved, to the satisfaction of our bodily needs and desires. How can we learn to overcome this ego? Should we give up all bodily satisfaction and live an ascetic life?

This is not the way of the Sufi. Since the Sufi aims at mastery and balance in life, we must learn to distinguish what the ego needs and what it does not need.

We can satisfy our natural needs; but we should avoid greed. We can enjoy the experiences of life, but without becoming attached and bound to them. Inayat Khan puts it extremely well:

> The training is to be wise in life, and to understand what we desire and why we desire it and what effect will follow, what we can afford and what we cannot afford. It is also to understand desire from the point of view of justice, to know whether it is right and just.[18]

The mental ego grows through attachment to our thoughts and feelings. If we identify with them, it follows naturally that we want our thoughts, feelings and actions – our personality – to be respected, even admired. This leads to vanity, which can have either negative or positive effects in our life. It works negatively when we belittle, even suppress and harm others in order to feel that we stand above them; this is vanity in a gross form. But a more refined form of vanity can motivate us to good deeds by which we hope to earn appreciation and respect from those around us. Most of us are dependent in many ways on the opinion of other people, whose appreciation thus feeds our vanity.

This mental ego is more difficult to train than the physical ego; it is subtler and more deeply engrained in our personality. To make progress in this training we must consciously analyze and evaluate our mental desires. We can then distinguish what our mental ego needs and what it does not. A certain natural satisfaction may be necessary to motivate us positively in our moral development. But exaggeration of our good qualities, through pride and conceit is not needed and will hamper our progress. The more we learn to control the mental ego, the more virtues will grow. In order to overcome this ego it is very helpful to become more conscious of God, the all-powerful creator who has given us all our good qualities and possibilities. Realizing this, our pride or conceit will melt away and be replaced by thankfulness for all the great gifts we have received in our life. An attitude of surrender to God will lead to modesty and humility. This humility can be practised 'by forgetting one's personality in every thought and action and in every dealing with another'. For then:

> The general tendency is to bring one's personality forward, which builds a wall between two souls whose destiny and happiness lies in unity. In business, in profession, in all aspects of life it is necessary that one should unite with the other in this unity, in which the purpose of life is fulfilled.[19]

In this way we can make progress on the Path. But the struggle will have to continue all the way. For when we have overcome certain vanities by a new modesty, our ego always tends to re-emerge in a finer form, as a subtler vanity. This is the meaning of Inayat Khan's saying in *The Gayan:*

'My modesty,/Thou art the veil that covers my subtle vanity'.[20] So we must continue to be watchful against this subtle enemy. For, as soon as this vanity revitalizes itself, it tends to limit us, to cut us off from divine inspiration and to restrict our heart.

When we continue the struggle to refine the mental ego, it can gradually be brought under control. Then the spiritual ego remains. What is this? Is this the real ego? We can see the spirit as the essence of our being. But becoming conscious of our inner being will still leave an ego – the highest form of ego: the ego of the spirit. For 'there is the spirit of man and the spirit of God. These two are different and yet the same. Think of the sea and of the bubble, how vast the one, how small the other!'[21]

Thus we can see that even as we reach the stage where we have purified the mirror of our mind and focussed it on our inner life, becoming conscious of the essence of our being, we still have one last jump to make: to become nothing, to forget ourselves completely and to immerse ourselves in the ocean of divine life. Moral evolution reaches its culmination and is fulfilled in mystical union with God: 'I am not, Thou alone art'.[22] Or, as the Zoroastrian scriptures put it: 'To Thee as sacrifice Zarathustra brings the very Life and Being of his Self'.[23]

That is the ultimate surrender of the spiritual ego to God. At the same time it is the third moral stage: the law of renunciation, where, as Inayat Khan says 'the difference of "mine" and "thine" and the distinction of "I" and "you" fade away in the realization of the one Life that is within and without, beneath and beyond; and that is the meaning of the verse in the Bible, "in Him we live and move, and have our being" '.[24]

10

The Mysticism of Sound

In chapter 5 we saw that the universe consists of vibrations of many different kinds. Among them the vibrations of sound play a most important role in the creation and in human life. They are very fine vibrations and are thus closest to the spirit. We have seen that the first stage of creation, called *wahdad*, when consciousness arose out of the Absolute, could be characterized as consciousness of sound. After that, in the further stage of manifestation, called *wahdaniyyat*, the sense of 'I exist' develops as the power of the Absolute concentrates, contracts. Then light is created which radiates into manifestation.[1] Thus: 'The unseen, incomprehensible, and imperceptible life becomes gradually known, by first becoming audible and then visible; and this is the origin and only source of all form'.[2] Inayat Khan further clarifies the role of sound in the creative process: 'Sound gives to the consciousness an evidence of its existence, although it is in fact the active part of consciousness itself which turns into sound. The knower, so to speak, becomes known to himself, in other words the consciousness bears witness to its own voice.'[3]

In this connection he often quotes the New Testament. 'In the beginning was the Word, and the Word was with God and the Word was God'.[4] But in reality this sound which was the beginning of the creation is the abstract sound. The vibrations of this sound are still finer, too fine to be audible to our material ears. This sound fills all space. It can be heard with the inner sense in deep meditation.[5]

After sound comes light; these two kinds of vibration manifest differently to us. Light, received by the eye, shows us the forms in the three-dimensional world, masking the illusory character of this material world behind the over-whelming clearness of what we see. Sound, received by our ear, is above form and can therefore more easily create a link for man with the spiritual world. In his interesting book, *Nada Brahma: The World of Sound*, Joachim Ernst Berendt describes our aural faculty as more female, yin, in character and the seeing faculty as male or yang.[6]

But this is only a difference in accent. Hazrat Inayat Khan even says: 'There is a relation between sound and colour. In reality they are one; they are two aspects of life. Life and light are one; life is light and light is life, and so colour is sound and sound colour. Only, when sound is colour it is most visible and least audible.'[7] And then he explains this: 'The very life which is audible is visible also; but where? It is visible on the inner plane.'[8] Thus, it is in the outer life that we distinguish light – with its colour – and sound, because we have different senses to perceive visible and audible things. But: 'In reality those who meditate, who concentrate, who enter within themselves, those who trace the origin of life, begin to see that behind these outer five senses there is one sense hidden.'[9]

Harmony and the creation

The combination of different tones or different colours in the right proportion and in the right rhythm creates harmony. Beauty is the result of harmony. We long for that beauty and therefore we always try to create harmony. The whole of creation also tends to harmony and is built on harmony. 'At the back of the whole creation is harmony, and the whole secret of création is harmony.'[10]

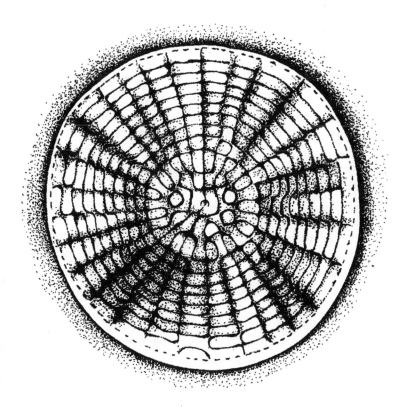

Figure 8 Pattern of sound waves, caused by moving along a steel plate

We are able to experience this harmony in the beauty of nature, where the singing of the birds and the rustling of the trees is as a divine music; and what indescribable beauty and harmony does unspoiled nature show to us with all its different shades of colour! This is the harmony we can all experience through our senses. But the wonderful thing is that the insight that modern science has gained into the secrets of the universe and the construction of the cosmos also unveils a breathtaking harmony. We touched on this in chapter 5, where we referred to 'The Music of the Spheres'.[11] We noted there that sound may be regarded as an abstract phenomenon, because tone is determined by the number of vibrations per second in any vibrating object. We can now add to this that chords, combinations of tones, are more harmonious the lower the number which describes the proportion of their vibrations. The octave, with a proportion 1:2 is the most harmonious; includes seven tones. The fifth, with a proportion of 2:3, and the fourth, 3:4, follow.[12]

These figures and proportions appear to characterize the harmonic structure of the micro- and macro-cosmos in different mathemetical variations. Thus, the building blocks of matter, the atoms, all have seven shells in which their electrons can circle around their nucleus. The quantum theory shows that electrons can move only in shells whose distances from the nucleus increase according to a geometric scale of 1, 4, 9 angstrom etc. (x^2).[13] The number of electrons that can have a place in these successive shells increases in a series of 2, 8, 18, $(2x^2)$.[14]

Finally, the speeds with which the electrons move in these successive shells show the proportion of 12 to 6 to 4 to 3 etc. and this corresponds exactly with the proportion between the vibrations in the most harmonious chords: 2:1, 3:2, 4:3.[15]

There seems to be a magic in these numbers! The secret of the creation indeed seems to be a remarkable harmony.

In the macrocosmos the distances of the planets from the sun conform approximately – but not exactly – to the mathematical progression: 4 + 0; 4 + 3; 4 + 6; 4 + 12 etc., again using similar proportions as in the musical consonants.[16]

Perhaps we can see a connection between this more approximate character of the macrocosmic harmony and the idea suggested by Berendt that the universe is 'aiming for harmony'. He points out that the planets cannot have varied their present orbits from the time of their origin. They must have 'found' these orbits out of the billions of possibilities after billions of years.[17] He adds that it took many hundreds of years to establish the system of musical harmonics. And in the world of nature every plant, every tree culminates in the blossoming from which its new seeds develop.

Thus the Creator has constructed the universe in an endless variety of harmonic relations. That harmony expresses the fundamental unity of the creation. The creative spirit must be working constantly to counter tendencies to disintegration and chaos that could develop according to logical analysis. All opposing forces and elements in the universe are kept together, embraced as they are by the Omnipresent Only Being which was their origin.

The parallelism that has been found between the harmonies in the universe and in music, has been expressed beautifully by Inayat Khan: 'Music is a miniature of the harmony of the universe, for the harmony of the universe is life itself.'[18] And thus, in making music one also aims at perfect harmony.

Meaning of sound in human life

Inayat Khan continues that passage as follows: 'And man, being a miniature of the universe, shows harmonious and inharmonious chords in his pulsation, in the beat of his heart, in his vibration, rhythm and tone. His health or illness, his joy or discomfort, all show the music or lack of music in his life.'[19] This brings us to the meaning of sound and of music in our life. The voice is our sound. For Inayat Khan this is the most living sound since its origin is in the breath. As we have seen in chapter 8, breath is spiritually very important. It links the spirit and the body; it is the life current.

So our words *can* be very meaningful, even powerful in our life. Very often though, in daily life we use so many words so superficially that their meaning depreciates; they become empty words. We know, nevertheless, that even words spoken unthinkingly can have a great psychological impact. If they suggest something positive – or negative – in our life, this can start us thinking and feeling along a certain line; and in this way a slight suggestion can bring about a significant effect in our life. It is necessary therefore to be conscious of the psychological effect of our words and to control them in a positive sense.

We know also that certain words can have a powerful effect that is immeasurably stronger than that of most words we use in daily life. This depends on the life behind the word, the strength and depth of the thought or feeling, the concentration or spiritual depth that it expresses. Inayat Khan tells us the illuminating story of a disciple who came to his teacher and started to ask a philosophical question. The spiritual teacher was, however, in deep meditation from which he would not be disturbed. He said to the disciple: 'Silence!' This word was so powerful that the disciple went into silence – and remained silent for the rest of his life. He never spoke again. However, as Inayat Khan tells us: 'There came a time when his silence began to speak aloud. His silent thought would manifest, and his silent wish would become granted; his silent glance would heal, his silent look would inspire. His silence became living.'[20]

If our voice and the words we speak can be so powerful, we should learn to use this wonderful instrument more consciously and positively in our life. This requires, in the first place, greater control of what we say. But this leads to the next question: how and in what direction should we use our words? For what purpose? And how can we then restore to them some of the power that they lose in our superficial daily use? Here we have to realize that, as Inayat Khan says, 'the voice is the expression of the spirit'.[21] It expresses the thoughts and feelings reflected in the soul. Therefore, it is not sufficient to control our words; we also have to control our thoughts and feelings, our moods, in the desired way. Otherwise friendly words will not sound convincing; our real feelings will show themselves in the tone of our voice, even while we are speaking friendly words. For this reason our voice can be used as a barometer, as Inayat Khan suggests. By consulting our voice, by listening to it, we can find out the real condition of our spirit.[22]

But we can also use the voice in spiritual practices, to influence our mind and deepen our consciousness. We touched on this when we mentioned the use of sacred words in chapter 8. Of course, our thoughts and feelings must be focussed on the sacred word as such, but pronouncing the word, with its vibration, can give great power to these practices.

This is the use of words in our inner life, where they regain some of their original power. To use our words in the right way in our outer life, we need to aim for harmony. This brings us in tune with the universe as it too is built on and tends to harmony. Thus, as we have already quoted from Inayat Khan, our joy or discomfort shows the music or lack of music in our life. Quoting him again: 'To obtain spirituality is to realize that the whole universe is one symphony; in this every individual is one note, and his happiness lies in becoming perfectly attuned to the harmony of the universe.'[23]

But how is it possible to remain in harmony with all around us when we meet so many disappointing people or people with differing views to which we cannot agree? The secret that opens the way to harmony is to widen our understanding, so that we begin to see the good of the bad in the mystical path of unlearning.[24]

In his book on music, Inayat Khan has described this process of unlearning:

> One would think that the character of the mind is such that what one learns is engraved upon it; how then can one unlearn it? Unlearning is completing this knowledge. To see a person and say, 'That person is wicked, I dislike him', that is learning. To

see further and recognize something good in that person, to begin to like him or to pity him, that is unlearning. When you see the goodness in someone whom you have called wicked, you have unlearned. You have unravelled that knot. First one learns by seeing with one eye; then one learns by seeing with two eyes, and that makes one's sight complete.[25]

This means rising beyond duality to unity. In musical terms one could see this as tuning ourselves to the fundamental tone which harmonizes with all other tones. In religious terms it means attuning our soul to God. Then every deed becomes music. And music helps us on the way to harmony in life. The enjoyment of music tunes one and puts one in harmony with life.[26]

Of all the arts music has a particular spiritual value and meaning because 'it helps man to concentrate or meditate independently of thought; and therefore music seems to be the bridge over the gulf between form and the formless'.[27] This is why music has always played an important role in Sufism, especially in the Chishtiyya school into which Inayat Khan was initiated. His vision of life is as a symphony. His teaching on music culminates in the following passage:

Beauty of line and colour can go so far and no further; the joy of fragrance can go a little further, but music touches our innermost being and in that way produces new life, a life that gives exaltation to the whole being, raising it to that perfection in which lies the fulfilment of man's life.[28]

One cannot help thinking here of the culmination of Inayat Khan's musical career in India, when – as we have seen in chapter 2 – he could reach the stage of *samadhi* in an instant. 'It developed to such an extent that not only he himself but those sitting around him would become spell-bound and feel exalted . . . After finishing his music Inayat was drowned in ecstasy and they all seemed as if lost in a mist.'[29]

11

Health and Healing

Rhythm and tone

Describing music as a miniature of the harmony of the whole universe, Hazrat Inayat Khan also teaches us that the harmonious or inharmonious cords in our pulsation, in our heart-beat, in our vibration, rhythm and tone determine our health or illness. His teachings on health start from this theme:

'Illness is an inharmony, either physical inharmony or mental inharmony, the one acts upon the other. What causes inharmony? The lack of tone and rhythm.'[1]

How should this musical analogy be interpreted? By 'tone' Inayat Khan means *prana*, life or energy. Lack of *prana* is weakness, physical and mental. Each person has his or her own particular tone, vibrating with the breath through the body. We must try to keep our tone at its proper pitch. The body, as a sacred instrument, must be kept in tune by 'carefulness in diet, by sobriety, and by breathing properly and correctly'.[2] And to keep the mental tone at the right pitch we must remain steady under life's changing conditions, by avoiding too much joy or too much sadness and by not changing moods too quickly.

'Rhythm' in the physical sense means regularity in circulation of the blood. We each have our own rhythm, peculiar to us. This must be maintained. Regularity in our habits, in action and repose, in everything, helps to give us 'that rhythm which is necessary and which completes the music of life'.[3] And we are warned that if our rhythm is broken for some reason it must be restored with great care, gradually, with wisdom and patience.

The rhythm of the mind is the action of the mind in harmonious or inharmonious thoughts: 'If one continues to think harmonious thoughts it is just like regular beating of the pulse.'[4] It is also the speed at which the mind works, which should be natural to the individual, neither jumping too quickly from one thought to another, nor brooding on one thought without making progress.[5]

Essential for maintaining the right rhythm, both physically and mentally, is balance between activity and repose. We have already touched on this in an earlier chapter. It means also that one cannot always give out energy: this could lead to exhaustion of the nerves. Another cause of this exhaustion is lack of sobriety: alcoholic and intoxicating substances of all kinds, as well as an excess of passion and anger, consume the energy of the nerves.[6]

Relation between mind and body

What is the relation between one's physical and mental condition? Broadly speaking Inayat Khan describes it in this way: 'The mind and the body stand face to face. The body reflects its order and disorder upon the mind, the mind reflecting at the same time its harmony and disharmony on the body.'[7] In *Metaphysics* he is able to be somewhat more precise: 'The mind makes a stronger impression upon the body, and the body makes a clearer impression upon the mind.'[8]

Imagination is an automatic working of the mind which can have a great influence on illnesses, often exaggerating pain or tiredness. It can even cause an illness or maintain it. As Inayat Khan says: 'Out of a hundred persons, sufferers from a certain illness, you will find ninety-nine who could be cured if their imagination allowed them to be cured.'[9] So illness may even disappear by withdrawing our imagination from it. Positive imagination can heal. All this shows once again how powerful the mind is and that control of the mind is the key to health and happiness.

Therefore we must develop positive thoughts to replace negative imaginations. Our nerves respond instantly to thought and transfer this influence to all parts of the physical body. This process is very clearly described by modern neuroscience. In his interesting book, *Quantum Healing*, Dr Deepak Chopra describes how the newly discovered neuro-transmitters travel to all parts of the body at incredible speeds.[10]

Of course, the influence of our thoughts depends on the strength and depth of the impulse of the mind. Here we must distinguish between thought and belief. One can think that one will be healed without really believing it at a deeper level. True belief is the best remedy against illness, although such belief is difficult, of course, when there is no supporting evidence. But here, as Inayat Khan points out: 'It is just like building a castle in the air, but then that castle becomes paradise'.[11]

Faith is the culmination of belief. Faith is felt in the deepest part of our being, where it creates an inner conviction that what one believes is going to happen. Faith is very powerful. 'Faith is so sacred that it cannot be imparted, it must be discovered within oneself.'[12] Faith is a grace of God. We can only open ourselves to it and trust in it. But to do that, we have to do away every kind of pessimistic outlook and feeling. Why can we have this trust? It is the spirit, the force of our divine soul, that works with the mind for a certain purpose. And 'as matter is the outcome of spirit, spirit has all power over matter'.[13]

When Inayat Khan gave us these teachings at the beginning of this century such beliefs seemed diametrically opposed to medical and scientific thinking. He noted this, saying: 'In the present age a person thinks that spirit is born of matter.' But recent advances in medical science have converged with the mystic's point of view. Dr Chopra puts it like this: 'Before this, science declared that we are physical machines that have somehow learned to think. Now it dawns that we are thoughts that have learned to create a physical machine.'[14]

Methods of healing

All this leads us to the subject of healing. Inayat Khan is extremely positive that we are able to achieve and maintain good health: 'There is no illness which is incurable; and we commit a sin against the perfection of the divine Being when we give up hope of any person's cure, for in that perfection nothing is impossible; all is possible.'[15] It is our duty to take good care of our body as it is 'an instrument that God created for his own experience'.[16] As to how we should do this – Inayat Khan takes a very balanced view. On the one hand we have to observe our health, our tone and rhythm, carefully, find the causes of disturbance and try to correct them, 'tuning ourselves'. On the other hand we must not think too much about our health, not allow our imagination to exaggerate and perhaps perpetuate any little problem. 'It is as necessary to take care of oneself as it is to forget about one's illness.'[17]

Inayat Khan also takes a balanced, though somewhat critical view, on traditional medical treatment. Speaking of medical techniques used to fight germs, bacteria and viruses he points out that, notwithstanding all the success these have, they may not always help. The reason is:

that everything that exists in the objective world has its living and more important part existing in the subjective world; and that part which is in the subjective is held by the belief of the patient. As long as the patient believes that he is ill he is giving sustenance to that part of the disease which is in the subjective world. Even if the germs of the disease were destroyed, not once but a thousand times in his body, they would be created there again.[18]

This idea is confirmed by Chopra:

According to Ayurveda, the conflict is being waged 'in here', contrary to the germ theory of disease, which tries to tell us that the war was started 'out there' by invaders of every kind – bacteria, viruses, carcinogens, et cetera – which are lying in wait to attack us. Yet healthy people live amid these dangers quite safely.[19]

With respect to drugs Inayat Khan warns that they are not always really successful; and that the aftereffects can be depleting and confusing for brain and mind. He acknowledges that drugs have their necessary place, but emphasizes that they should not be used for little things that can be cured by other means.[20] But, as he says in a later passage, 'if a disease can be cured with a simple remedy the mental power should not be wasted, for it may be used in a more serious case. If every malady were to be healed mentally then why were all drugs and herbs created?'[21] So it is a balance in the application of the different techniques that is needed. Dr Chopra also comes to the conclusion that our modern insight 'makes drugs look much more dangerous than we had thought'.[22] Surgical operations can also be of real assistance, but the aftereffects on the nervous system are so serious that they should not be undertaken lightly.[23]

Inayat Khan attaches great importance to overcoming illness and expresses this very clearly. Should illness or death not be seen as being the will of God? 'Death is different from illness, for illness is worse than death. The sting of death is only momentary; the idea that one leaves one's surroundings is one moment's bitter experience, no longer; but illness is incompleteness, and that is not desirable.'[24] This leads to two important pronouncements concerning euthanasia, a subject on which there is much controversy at the present time. First, he says that doctors should not kill in order to save a person from pain, 'for nature is wise, and every moment that one passes on this physical plane has its purpose. We human beings are too limited to judge, to decide to put an end to life and suffering.' We must, however, try to diminish the suffering. On the other hand,

> to use artificial means of keeping someone alive for hours or days is not a right thing to do; because that is going against nature's wisdom and the divine plan. It is as bad as killing a person. The tendency is for man always to go further than he ought to; that is where he makes a mistake.[24]

Considering all the limitations of medicine: drugs and operations, which is the best way to good health? 'The best medicine is a pure diet, nourishing food, fresh air, regularity in action and repose, clearness of thought, pureness of feeling, and confidence in the perfect Being, with whom we are linked and whose expression we are.'[25]

Spiritual healing

It is that confidence in the perfect Being of God that makes us receptive to the divine gift of faith. Then the all-powerful spirit can work to heal us from any illness. Prayer is helpful in this process, because it makes us conscious of our inner link to the Divine Being. In meditation we can come in direct contact with the pure intelligence and power of our soul, the divine spirit within us; that is the source of the most perfect healing. In an unpublished teaching Hazrat Inayat Khan has explained this as follows:

The meditative process is a treatment for all illnesses. The reason is that the manifested life comes from the unmanifested. The unmanifested life is void of all activity and is full of repose; it is peace in itself . . .

No remedy therefore is greater than peace.

Medicines can help, but up to a certain limit. For instance medicine can help the body, but not the mind; psychological treatment may help the mind, but not the soul. All these things such as medicine and psychological treatment come from outside and the patient is dependent upon them, but in the meditative process the patient creates his remedy from himself.[26]

Furthermore, as vibrations are behind everything in the universe as well as within man, the 'power of the word' can have a strong healing effect. By this Inayat Khan also means vibrations, including music. In this context, we are told that there was a physician in America who had this idea and followed it up scientifically.[27] This physician probably was Dr Abrams, who invented radionics, the use of electrical vibrations for healing. Inayat Khan refers to him elsewhere and with great hope about this medical development:

He began to get some good results, but it is a subject which will need at least a century to develop fully. It is a vast subject and this is just a beginning; therefore there is still no end to the errors; but at the same time, if people could bear with it, after many years something might come out of it which could be of great use to the medical world.[28]

At one time the technique of radionics was heavily criticized in the medical world, but now it seems to be gaining wider acceptance, especially in Britain. Healing by meditation and sound is also used in the modern development of the ancient Ayurvedic medicine. Dr Chopra, who studied these ancient methods scientifically, at the request of Maharishi Mahesh Yogi, has explained how the technique of transcendental meditation, the so-called 'Bliss technique' and primordial sound can have a powerful healing influence.[29] These are all ways of self-healing which Inayat Khan sees as more desirable than healing by others, because it strengthens the will.[30]

But often we need another's help. Inayat Khan explains how we can help others by spiritual healing, comparing the difference between medicine and spiritual healing with travel by rail or by air.[31]

Health – our tone and rhythm – is a vibration. Faith and meditation create a fundamental harmonious vibration which is the most perfect healing. Such vibrations are not confined merely within our own mind and body; they can be received by other people and can be purposively directed to people who need healing. These vibrations are created and transmitted by the breath and can be directed in different ways. These are:

> healing by writing a sacred word;
> by magnetising water;
> by waving the hands over the affected part of the person's body;
> by touch;
> by glance;
> by the power of the voice giving a suggestion;
> by presence with sympathy;
> by prayer;
> and finally there is absent healing, where the healing vibrations can bridge any distance. This is a very different method of healing.[32]

This healing power can be explained as follows:

> Breath, so to speak, is an electric current that can be attached anywhere; distance makes no difference. A current of breath so established puts the ethereal waves in space into motion, and according to the healer's magnetic power the space between the healer and the patient becomes filled with a running current of healing power. There is no doubt that spiritual evolution is the first thing necessary; without this the mind-power of a healer,

however strong, is too feeble for the purpose. By spiritual development is meant God-consciousness.[33]

This brings us to the core of the question as to how spiritual healing power can be developed. Spiritual development is mentioned below in general terms, while it is explained at greater length in chapter 8. First, the power of breath must be developed by spiritual breathing practices. Next, the healer must be in the right rhythm and he must have reached purity of mind. Then concentration is needed, with sympathy for the ill person; the concentration must not focus on the pain or illness but on the renewal of health. Finally, and most important, is belief in God: the healer must become a channel for the divine healing power. Inayat Khan says here:

> When the healer thinks he is healing, his power is as small as a drop; when he thinks God is healing, and when owing to this thought his own self is forgotten and he is only conscious of the self of God, then his power becomes as large as the ocean.[34]

This is made still clearer in the following inspiring passage:

> It is the belief and realization that, 'I do not exist, but God', which gives power to the healer to heal from a distance; also it is this realization that gives him the belief that his thought can reach to any distance, because the knowledge of the all-pervading God gives him the realization that the Absolute is life in itself, and that even space, which means nothing to the average person, is everything; in fact, it is the very life of all things.[35]

The mystical healers have shown through the ages what spiritual healing can do. Inayat Khan himself was a great healer but he felt that he had to give most of his time to developing and spreading the Sufi message. Murshid Ali Khan, his cousin, who followed him from the beginning of his work for the Sufi message and who was spiritual head and Representative General of the Sufi movement from 1948 to 1958, developed a wonderful healing power and has devoted himself whole-heartedly to this task. He is an example of the different qualities needed for healing: his breath was very powerful, he had great purity, deep sympathy and an unshakeable belief in God. He was also a great master of music, tone and vibration.

Murshid Ali Khan used to say, when somebody thanked him for being healed, while raising his hands upwards, 'it is only thanks to God'. There have been some remarkable instances of his healing among the friends and followers of the Sufi message. Hazrat Inayat Khan considered the development of spiritual healing to be so important that he created a separate activity of spiritual healing in the Sufi movement. Initiates participating in this healing activity meet regularly in small groups to practise absent healing. A simple ritual with special prayers and meditations is given for this purpose. It is a modest and invisible way of working to help those who are suffering pain or illness.

12

The Ideal of Peace: Some Social Aspects

Inner peace

In previous chapters I have tried to describe some of the beauties of Hazrat Inayat Khan's Universal Sufism: its mystical philosophy; its vision of the voyage of the human soul; its universal religious worship; its inner school; and the mysticism of sound and its relation to our health. All this can help us to find our personal way through the difficulties and complexities of life in the direction of our ultimate purpose. But the question now arises: how can the Sufi ideal help to bring peace to the world, to our still divided, fighting and suffering world?

We have seen how both moral evolution and spiritual growth lead us to the deeply satisfying experience of peace in our heart. This is the greatest blessing. As Inayat Khan says in the *Gayan*: 'Verily, the heart that receives the divine Peace is blessed'.[1] And in the *Aphorisms* he describes this inner peace as follows:

> Peace is not a knowledge, peace is not a power, peace is not a happiness; yet peace is all these. Besides, peace is productive of happiness, peace inspires one with knowledge of the seen and unseen, and in peace is to be found the Divine Presence.[2]

The path that can lead us to this peace in our heart is taken by controlling and overcoming our false ego.

In Sufi terminology this false ego is the *nafs*. An unpublished series of teachings inspired by Hazrat Inayat Khan, 'The Book of Peace'[3] starts from this concept: 'As all wars are caused by activity of the *nafs*, so all forms of peace arise from control of *nafs*, and this is true whether considered from the universal or particular standpoint.' This *nafs*, the false ego, is formed – as we have seen[4] – by our identification with our limited being, our body and mind, and all the needs, thoughts and emotions that live in it. The key to Inayat Khan's approach to world peace, now, is that this need to control the *nafs* 'is true, whether considered from the universal or particular standpoint'. Thus we can look at the

> *nafs* of a person – as we have been doing until now – but also at the
> *nafs* of a social ideal,
> *nafs* of a nation and
> *nafs* of a religion or belief.

In these cases it is also the identification of a social group or organization with a limited ideal; of a people with its limited national characteristics and interests; and of a church or religious organization with its particular form of belief. In all these cases peace is dependent on control of this *nafs*. We will therefore look at each of these different forms of *nafs* or illusory identification in turn.

The *nafs* of a person has already been discussed in chapter 9, on moral culture. There is one further aspect in 'The Book of Peace' which illuminates and complements the earlier argument. To begin with we are warned that the *nafs* is a very treacherous animal: 'Many can speak against the *nafs*, whereas unless inspired to speak, unless such speech arises from the heart, the tongue is controlled by *nafs*.' There is always a temptation to attack the *nafs* of another person; and even if the *nafs* turns upon itself, 'it is strengthening itself, which is very deceiving'. Therefore 'the way of the Sufis is to lull the devil to sleep rather than rouse him to wakefulness because of opposition.'

By this is meant: do not occupy your mind with fighting unrighteousness, but rather cultivate goodness. Focussing the mind on friendly and loving thoughts and feelings brings that goodness to life in us. For – as we have seen – the mind is creative. Thoughts and feelings to which we give attention grow, become stronger and lead to further positive feelings and actions. Inayat Khan often compares our mind to a garden which we have to cultivate. Opposition to unrighteousness is then seen as, 'pulling weeds from a garden where one is not so sure they may not grow again. Cultivating righteousness is the implanting of flowers or trees which will choke out of the weeds by themselves.' The conclusion is: 'As opposition to unrighteousness sometimes leads to self-righteousness, the cultivation of the heart qualities is often the superior way, and the path of the saint is generally preferable to that of the prophet or master.'

This last quotation also stresses the importance of the heart qualities. In our thoughts – on the surface of our mind – we always have to distinguish and analyze differences and this easily stimulates the *nafs*; we identify with our own particular ideas. It is the deeper feelings in the heart, feelings of love, friendship, forgiveness and so on which lead us to overcome differences and experience unity. This is essential in our individual spiritual development.

But this individual evolution is also of fundamental importance for society and for the world. The state of evolution of all human beings determines the climate in which political leaders take the decisions which can lead to war or peace. For all our thoughts and feelings have a certain life in what C G Jung calls the 'collective unconscious'. They are received – consciously or unconsciously – by other minds and influence them.

In this way each person makes a contribution to war or peace in the world. Therefore our first responsibility – if we want to work for peace – is to create peace in our own heart. As Inayat Khan says in the *Gayan*: 'O peace-maker, before trying to make peace throughout the world, first make peace within thyself!'

The eternal world and the temporal

This is a simple but very important recommendation. For it is by making peace in our own heart that we open the way to experience the unity and perfection of God; it is this experience that we all long for. But when we cannot see clearly what the spiritual character of this perfection is we become confused and try to reach perfection on earth, rather than creating it in our hearts. Both Walter Lippmann and Aldous Huxley have warned us forcibly not to confuse the two worlds of the spirit and of the earth, the eternal world and the temporal world.

Walter Lippmann distinguishes two 'realms': the 'realm of the material world, where the human condition is to be born, to live, to work, to struggle and to die' and the 'realm of essence', that of the 'transcendent world in which man's soul can be regenerate and at peace'.[5] In a similar way Aldous Huxley sees two opposed philosophies: one 'which affirms the existence and the immediate realizableness of *eternity*'; and one 'which affirms that which goes on *in time* as the only reality'.[6]

What it is important to recognize is that the perfection, the salvation that man is longing for in the depth of his heart, can be found only in the realm of the transcendent world of the spirit, of eternity; that is to say, within our own deepest being, our soul. The realm of the material world, the world of time, is very different. Life in this world is limited, temporary and imperfect; full of conflict and contradiction, confusion and complication. There is no absolute good in this world; all is relative. It is impossible here to give clear and general prescriptions. Aristotle has warned us that we cannot find the right rule if we look for more 'clearness' than the subject matter admits of.[7]

Thus, Walter Lippmann continues, the wisdom of the Bible 'does not contain the systematic and comprehensive statement of moral principles from which it is possible to deduce with clarity and certainty specific answers to concrete questions'.[8]

In the political world we see confirmation of this in the great changes that the programmes of Christian parties have undergone in the course of time, and in the number of similarities with programmes of non-religious parties. It is very clear that economic policy belongs to this material realm. Therefore it cannot bring us the perfection that we seek. Economic science shows that for the vast majority of people material resources are always scarce in relation to our growing needs. The economic optimum consists of a careful balancing of these scarcities: allocating our resources in such a way over different uses that the greatest total utility or satisfaction is achieved. But this is not perfection. And – since incentives are needed to stimulate people to contribute to the national product – income differences are inevitable, so that there are great variations in the degree of satisfaction that different individuals are able to reach, which can conflict with our feeling for justice. Experience shows that this can to some extent be mitigated, but never eliminated without causing misery for all. Indeed, as Lippmann puts it: 'As the bitter end has become visible in the countries of the total revolution, we can see how desperate is the predicament of modern men. The terrible events show that the harder they try to make earth into heaven, the more they make it a hell.'[9]

It is very clear then that perfection – perfect justice – is not possible in a material world. But this does not mean that we should withdraw from the world and leave it, fatalistically, to its miserable devices in order to focus on a meditative life in a monastery or in an Indian *ashram*. It makes a great difference in the human condition whether societies are governed in a reasonable fashion by sensible leaders who have the wellbeing of the people in mind, so that within the framework of reasonable laws a sufficient scope for free deployment of human energy is possible, leading to an acceptable level of welfare. A minimum of material means and of freedom will also create better conditions, in which many people can then turn their attention to the spiritual path, where our deepest longings can be fulfilled.

This is why the Sufi ideal of balance between the inner and outer life is so important. When we can draw strength and inspiration from the perfect source within, we can work in the right spirit in the imperfect world outside.

In that spirit one will have a wider outlook, so that all the different aspects of a problem and all the consequences of certain actions can be carefully evaluated. Then one can more easily find the correct middle way, the wise compromise in which opposing interests or points of view can be peacefully brought together. Such a balanced attitude is suggested in the following passage from 'The Book of Peace':

> The question as to whether Sufis may favor such movements as the prohibition of liquor, dope and vice is very difficult to answer, because what seems a simple question is a very complex question put into a few words. There may be several moral and spiritual issues at stake, and before deciding it is proper to analyze all of them. This does not mean neutrality, although it does not exclude neutrality and it is not opposed to neutrality. It means examine all principles first, see from all points of view, but do not hesitate to favor a cause you feel is morally or spiritually right.[10]

'The Book of Peace' also underlines the need of sobriety, indicating at the same time that this is not easy and requires some sacrifice for a mystic.

Sobriety is an attitude which is always necessary when a problem is at hand. Mystics are not always sober, for the practice of the presence of God is very stimulating to the heart and mind and leads to spiritual intoxication or ecstasy. But when a problem is at hand man's duty is to serve God rather than to search for Him. In serving in humility and modesty one may be serving God without being aware of His presence.[11]

All this, of course, means controlling the *nafs* of our limited social ideals or purposes, as the *nafs* would close our mind to other aspects and thus could lead to disharmony and conflict.

Peace among nations

What about peace in the world at large? Conflicts and large-scale wars between different nations have caused immense suffering and damage to humanity in the past and could be totally devastating in the future if nuclear arms were ever used. It is vital, therefore, for the world to find a way to a more peaceful co-existence of nations.

What is the Sufi approach to this in 'The Book of Peace'? Following Immanuel Kant's inspiring treatise, *Towards Eternal Peace*, it starts with a comparison between the individual and the nation:

> The problem of the nation is not so different from the problem of the individual, only on a grand scale. There are two aspects to the personality: that soul which is an accomodation for God to touch the life on the surface and is really nothing but God, and that collection of thoughts, ideas, emotions and sensations attached to name. So nationality has two aspects: that accomodation for a group of individuals over a larger or smaller area to act as a unit, and that series of acts, ideas and ideals attached to the government, laws and industry of the same area.[12]

In this sense we can indeed think of a national mind which, as Jung's 'collective unconscious', has been created by the total experience, thoughts, feelings and ambitions of a nations' inhabitants. Such a nation therefore has its own vital identity that cannot be disregarded and dissolved in order to create one world under one world government. We can see great progress in the development of nations:

> It has required ages to build the family and clan into the tribe and the tribe into the nation. This was not a rapid or an easy process. Man, forgetful of the past and troubled by the present, with an eye on the future, does not always take into account the many difficult stages passed through to build even the types of government which exist today. With all their faults and short-comings, when one looks upon the past there seems to be so much improvement. One can see there something of the evolution of the whole human race, slow though that be.[13]

Kant also sees this development of the nation as an important achievement to which humanity is led by nature. Nature he calls 'the great artist' that lets cooperation and unity grow from the differences and conflicts created by man; and he recognizes in this 'nature' – 'the fundamental wisdom which found its cause in a higher idea directed to the final destination of humanity'.[14]

We could, therefore, regard his 'nature' as the divine spirit of guidance. Similarly Charles Darwin has recognized a 'natural law of co-operation' besides his law of survival of the fittest. He sees that:

> as man advances in civilization, and small tribes are united into larger communities, the simplest reason would tell each individual that he ought to extend his social instincts and sympathies to all members of the same nation, though personally unknown to him . . . this point being once reached, there is only an artificial barrier to prevent his sympathies extending to the men of all nations and races.[15]

Kant then observes that in the course of time a people begins to understand that it is in its members' interest to work together and to keep to certain rules governing their mutual relationships, instead of individual families or towns fighting against each other. For this purpose a legal system develops, which protects each citizen from violence, while courts of justice are created to resolve conflicts and differences. A certain balance between contradicting interests is then created. In a similar way nations must learn to live together in peace. For that purpose international rules of law have to be developed and accepted, which protect all nations against possible violence and aggression by their neighbours. An international court of justice then becomes necessary in order to settle differences between them. In this way all nations can learn to cooperate.

The world is now trying to cope with this task through the United Nations and its various agencies but it has proved a very difficult task. Trying to reach an agreement on urgent international issues between a large number of independent nations, each with their different and often passionately defended views, can be extremely frustrating. It requires a great deal of energy, patience and perseverence. What is essential for success is that the different national delegations learn to listen to each other's arguments. This can then lead to a widening of outlook, a greater understanding, so that a consensus can be reached. A certain control of the *nafs* of the nation is needed in order to accept such a common consensus which only partially reflects any one nation's own ideas and interests.

Integration of the world economy

Kant tells us that economic and financial interests will lead nations to cooperate. This argument has gradually become stronger. In the past, economic interests often conflicted and have sometimes led to war. But in the present century an increasingly integrated world economy is developing. International trade has increased enormously under the influence of ever-cheaper transport and communications. This makes national economies more and more dependent on each other. The existence of international financial markets also creates close links between national economies.

Large capital-flows establish mutual financial interests and connect rates of interests in national capital markets. In many respects national economies have become parts of one world economy. It is becoming more and more difficult therefore for national governments to control their economies autonomously. International economic and monetary cooperation between governments becomes more and more necessary in many fields. A number of international organizations have been doing important work in this field. In my view, the World Bank and the IMF have been particularly valuable. Since the end of the Second World War they have been set up in such a way that decisions are taken on the basis of a majority of votes. This means that, within the limited area of their responsibility, an element of national sovereignty has been transferred to them. This was only possible because the voting system is realistically based on the economic size of member nations. These institutions have also been able to work efficiently as they are governed by an executive board of no more than 24 members elected by the 177 member countries on the basis of their voting power. In fact the executive board very seldom votes but nearly always aims for a consensus. This way of working makes it necessary for all executive directors and the chairman to listen very carefully to the different arguments brought forward, to weigh their validity and importance. The importance of a decision reached by consensus is that it avoids forcing a limited but powerfully defended view (the *nafs* of a national view) on all; instead differing points of view are accommodated in a reasonable equilibrium.

In a number of cases these institutions have done valuable work for the world economy, although many important decisions still have to be negotiated bilaterally or in a small group of the major nations. Nevertheless the discussions in the so-called Group of 5 and Group of 7 of the main industrial countries represent a step forward in international cooperation and have brought about better understanding and some positive results in coordination of policies. It is to be hoped that this cooperation can in time be widened into a world economic council.[16]

These developments are encouraging, but compared to the enormous need for international cooperation in the present world, they represent only a modest beginning. Even in fields where an urgent need for cooperation is clear, it remains difficult to persuade public opinion and parliaments in the developed democracies to subordinate narrow national interest to the common good of all nations. At the same time some violent conflicts and small-scale wars have broken out between and within developing countries, which are often governed by dictatorships.

There is thus a great need for wider understanding and support of peaceful cooperation. How can this be brought about? 'The Book of Peace' considers various elements that could bring people together.

Unifying elements

Idealistic people have hoped that one international language could be created that would help to unite mankind. But the attempt to do this through the artificial language of Esperanto has failed to gain acceptance. What is needed is a 'language of the heart'. 'The Book of Peace' refers to the story of the tower of Babel where the differences in language sprang up: 'The word "Babel" means "gate of God". It is only at God's threshold that one language is spoken, and this is the language of the heart. The true Babel or threshold of God is not on the physical plane but on the heart plane. Its universal language is not speech but music.'[17]

Babel in Hebrew or *bab-ilu* in Babylonian indeed means 'gate of God'. But *balal* means 'to confuse' and is pronounced similarly, so that the text of Genesis 9:1–9 can connect this with the confusion of languages which originated there.[18]

Music will be the only universal language; already 'the whole world today is listening in some form to the music of other races, other peoples, other civilizations; and not only listening but often appreciating it'. But for music to be a truly unifying element for all men, it has to be universal. As national anthems 'have served to unite all the people of a country', so music inspired by a universal divine ideal could help to bring together the whole of humanity. We can be inspired here by Inayat Khan's perception and his own experience of music as the highest – because most abstract – way of aesthetic contemplation. It comes closer to mystical meditation and realization than any other human aspiration and creativity.

Common ideals can also bring people in many nations together; here we can think of forest protection, the preservation of whales and similar movements. The dangers to our environment, which have become so clear, are now indeed giving great power to such movements. 'Within man there is strong will to peace, an echo or reflection from his true nature. Every once in a while it appears in some movement of co-operation with his fellow man.'[19] In recent years this tendency has been demonstrated most impressively in the Peace Movement, which draws a strong emotional force from the perceived and terrible danger of a nuclear war. However, in one's 'zeal for international brotherhood' one should not become intolerant to those whose horizons are less wide.

Can science, which is of its nature universal, help to bring people together, thus making it easier to maintain peace?

'The Book of Peace' points out the limitations of science in this respect: 'Even scientists realize the defect of science as a universal ideal. In addition to it being the handmaiden of war it requires considerable intelligence to understand its deeper principles, so it may take a long time to reach the hearts and minds of most people.'[20] But then it is also foreseen that: 'Sooner or later the scientists will begin to investigate consciousness, to study more deeply physic and mental phenomena, and this will bring them to accept the existence of worlds beyond our senses.'[21]

This development in science is also becoming increasingly important at the present time. It inspires many spiritual currents in the so-called New Age movement with its holistic philosophy. All this contributes to greater unity and brotherhood.

Need for universal religion

Inayat Khan feels strongly, however, that the religious aspect is also needed:

> The brotherhood of man without the Fatherhood of God is like a body without blood. The form may be there, but there will be no life in it. All the precepts and commandments cannot unite people whose hearts are not melted to flow like rivers into each other and to empty into that all-embracing sea of life which is God.[22]

What the world needs then is a universal religious awareness. This means that the *nafs* of religion must also be conquered: This is an exclusive identification with particular forms of belief and ritual which are seen as representing the only way to God, to salvation. Such believers demand that others accept the same belief and ritual and this often leads to conflict rather than peace. In reality belief and ritual are the means which can help us, ways along which man can develop his religious life. The many different ways of the great religions are all converging to the one divine reality that has to be experienced. Cooperation between religions is therefore very valuable: 'Every amalgamation of churches, regardless of loss of membership, is a movement towards peace'.[23]

For this purpose Inayat Khan created the Universal Worship as the religious activity of the Sufi movement. In this Universal Worship all great religions come together: the ritual symbolizes how the divine light has come through them to humanity; and by reading from their sacred scriptures we can experience the harmony between their different ways of worshipping the divine being and of expressing the one moral ideal of love, compassion and tolerance between men. That is the basis for peace in the world.

A Prayer for Peace

Send Thy Peace, O Lord, which is perfect and everlasting, that our souls may radiate peace.

Send Thy Peace, O Lord, that we may think, act and speak harmoniously.

Send Thy Peace, O Lord, that we may be contented and thankful for Thy Bountiful Gifts.

Send Thy Peace, O Lord, that amidst our worldly strife we may enjoy Thy Bliss.

Send Thy Peace, O Lord, that we may endure all, tolerate all in the thought of Thy Grace and Mercy.

Send Thy Peace, O Lord, that our lives may become a divine vision, and in Thy Light all darkness may vanish.

Send Thy Peace, O Lord, our Father and Mother, that we, Thy Children on earth, may all unite in one brotherhood.

Conclusion

In the previous chapters I have described some important aspects of Universal Sufism, the Sufi message of Hazrat Inayat Khan. But as I warned in the Preface, such a description will inevitably be insufficient. The Sufi message is rich and all-embracing; there are more aspects to it than could be adequately covered in the context of this book.

The core of the Sufi message is mysticism, the inner path. In the Sufi Order, the Sufi Movement's Esoteric School of Inner Culture, Inayat Khan has entrusted to his *mureed*s an incredible treasure of spiritual practices which are considered by the initiates as a sacred and secret trust given to them for their personal growth. In addition Inayat Khan has given a wealth of more esoteric teachings which are meant especially for his *mureed*s, as they progress to higher initiations. These teachings therefore have not been published. The art of spiritual discipleship is an important part of these very subtle teachings.

The Inner School is also the core activity of the Sufi Movement, the organization which Inayat Khan founded in 1923 in Geneva to protect and spread the Sufi message. Although as a mystic he did not like organizational and administrative matters, he saw that his spiritual message needed an organizational body to survive in the material world, just as the human soul needs its physical body to be able to live on earth. Of course, this organization is only an instrument serving the spiritual ideal of Sufism. To prevent this organization developing material interests and becoming to some extent a purpose in itself, there is no professional priesthood. The work in the organization and in its different activities, even that of the authorized initiators, is done on a voluntary basis by the *mureeds* who do this besides their worldly tasks. This is also consistent with the ideal of balance between inner and outer work.

The structure of the Sufi Movement is hierarchical in a way that Inayat Khan himself has clearly indicated. This reflects the character of the spiritual relationship and attitude needed in its central activity: the Sufi Order, the Inner School. This structure is intended to enable the inspiration of the spiritual leader of the Sufi Movement to pervade and guide the whole organization. At the same time, in various councils and committees, the views of those who work in the movement can be fully represented and expressed, so that the spiritual leader can take them into account.

The old Sufi tradition was built entirely on discipleship and consisted mainly in esoteric training. Naturally therefore it developed into a large number of Sufi Orders, circles of disciples around different spiritual teachers. *Mureed*ship is a very personal relationship, so that one must be free to choose one's teacher.

The modern Sufi Movement, as established by Hazrat Inayat Khan, is not only an Inner School but an organization built in order to spread the ideals of Universal Sufism in the world at large. For this work, great unity of all who work for these ideals is important. At the present time a balance has been found between the necessary freedom to choose one's spiritual leader and the need for unity in the Sufi work, as different spiritual leaders with their *mureed*s work together in the Sufi Movement at the same time as cooperation has been established between the Sufi Movement (under the spiritual guidance of Pir-o-Murshid Hidayat Inayat Khan,

Hazrat Inayat Khan's second son), the Sufi Order International (created by Pir Vilayat Inayat Khan, Hazrat Inayat Khan's eldest son) and the Sufi Islamia Ruhaniat Society (that is now developing a very close contact to the Sufi Movement).

Every organisation exists as a human activity and therefore it is always to some extent imperfect. But behind the Sufi organizations is the inspiring and radiating spirit of Hazrat Inayat Khan. And Inayat Khan always emphasized to his *mureed*s – who naturally were almost blinded by the radiance of his inspiration – that they should see and understand the Sufi message behind his personality. Beyond its expression in Inayat Khan's teachings and in the activities of the Sufi movement is the invisible stream of inspiration that is working in the conscience of humanity and manifests itself in a rich variety of ways. Behind that is the divine reality. As Inayat Khan has said: 'The messenger is a veil over the message, and the message is a veil over God.'

Notes

Chapter 1

1 Quoted by A J Arberry, *An Introduction To the History of Sufism*, Longman, Green, London, 1942, p 44.
2 For further data on this see L Hoyack in *De Soefi Gedachte*, June 1954.
3 In A J Arberry, *Sufism: An Account of the Mystics of Islam*, London, 1950, pp 52–3.
4 L Hoyack, 'De Wijsheid van Hermes Trismegistos', in *De Soefi Gedachte*, September 1954, p 66 (quoted from H Brugsch, *Religion und Mythologie der alten Egypter*).
5 *The Sufi Message of Inayat Khan*, II, p 202.
6 Hoyack, 'De Wijsheid', p 68.
7 *The Sufi Message*, X, p 203.
8 ibid, *IX*, p 173.
9 ibid, p 173.
10 ibid, p 174.
11 Quoted in *Emergence, Journal for Evolving Consciousness*, 1, p 8.
12 ibid, p 8.
13 See the penetrating analysis by R C Zaehner in his *Hindu and Muslim Mysticism*.
14 Arberry, *Sufism*, p 36.
15 ibid, p 37.
16 R A Nicholson, *The Mathnavi of Jelal-ud-Din Rumi*, E. J. W. Gibb Memorial Series, Lucas, London, 1972, p 5.
17 *The Sufi Message*, X, p 141.

18 *Complete Works of Pir-o-Murshid Hazrat Inayat Khan, original texts: Lectures on Sufism 1923, 1, January–June*, East–West Publications, London/The Hague, 1989, p 145.

19 *Mystical Poems of Rumi*, translated by A J Arberry, University of Chicago Press London, 1968, p 11.

20 ibid, pp 18–19.

21 ibid, pp 9–10.

22 ibid, p 30.

23 *Poems from the Divan of Hafiz*, Javidan Publication, 1963, p 25.

24 ibid, p 65.

25 ibid, p 34.

26 *The Bustan of Saadi*, The Wisdom of the East Series, John Murray London, 1911, p 23.

27 *The Sufi Message*, XI, p 115.

28 *The Gulistan or Rose Garden of Saadi*, translated by Edward Rehatsek, George Allen & Unwin, London, 1964, p 105.

29 ibid, pp 88–9.

30 See Arberry, *An Introduction to Sufism*, pp vi–x.

31 This Order was founded by two earlier members of the Suhrawardia family, not the great Shihabuddin Yahya al Suhrawardi mentioned on p 5.

32 W D Begg, *The Holy Biography of Hazrat Khwaja Muin-ud-Din Chishti*, W D Begg, Ajmer, 1960, p 51.

33 ibid, p 107.

34 ibid, p 113.

35 See Zahurul Hassan Sharib, *Khwaja Gharib Nawaz*, p 97.

Chapter 2

1 The material for this chapter is taken from Part I of the *Biography of Pir-o-Murshid Inayat Khan*, East–West Publications, London/The Hague, 1979. References in the text are shown as (*B*, p...).

2 Some interesting material on Maula Bakhsh's motivations and aims in his search for musical reform and development can be found in E de Jong-Keesing, *Inayat Khan: A Biography*, East–West Publications, London/The Hague, 1974.

3 There are colourful additional descriptions of the life and mood

in Baroda at the time in *Murshid* Musharaff Khan's memoir, *Pages in the Life of a Sufi*, Sufi Publishing Company, 1971.

4 *Murshid* is the Indian word for spiritual guide. *Pir-o-Murshid* (Eldest Teacher and Guide) is the leader of the spiritual school. The disciples are called *mureeds*.

5 The *vina* is an Indian musical instrument similar to a guitar, but has two large gourds, one at each end.

Chapter 3

1 The material for the first part of this chapter is taken from Part II of the *Biography of Pir-o-Murshid Inayat Khan*, East–West Publications, London/The Hague, 1979. Page references are given as in the previous chapter.

2 E. de Jong-Keesing, *Inayat Khan: a Biography*, East–West Publications, The Hague/London, 1974, p 122.

3 This is dealt with at greater length in chapter 11.

4 *The Flower Garden of Inayat Khan*, East–West Publications, The Hague/London, 1978, p 10.

5 From the 1982 commemorative issue of the Dutch magazine *De Soefi Gedachte*, pp 51–3.

6 S van Stolk and D Dunlop, *Memories of a Sufi Sage: Hazrat Inayat Khan*, East–West Publications, London/The Hague, 1967, pp 62–3.

7 ibid, p 6.

8 *Forty Years of Sufism (Sufi Quarterly Special Issue)*, 1950, p 47.

9 Commemorative issue, *De Soefi Gedachte*, pp 45–8.

10 A place near Paris where Hazrat Inayat Khan then lived and gave his first summer school in 1921.

11 Aquarelle: a painting in watercolour, sometimes with pencil or ink.

12 Commemorative issue, *De Soefi Gedachte*, pp 30–31.

Chapter 4

1 *The Sufi Message of Inayat Khan*, X, pp 130–31.

2 A J Arberry, *Sufism: An Account of the Mystics of Islam*, George, Allen & Unwin, London, 1950, pp 134–5.

3 *The Sufi Message* VIII, pp 20–21.

Chapter 5

1 F Capra, *The Turning Point*, Wildwood House, London, 1982, p 76.
2 *The Sufi Message* XI, p 25.
3 *The Kybalion*, Yogi Publication Society, Chicago, 1908, p 137.
4 Guy Murchie, *Music of the Spheres*, II, Dover, New York, 1967.
5 *The Sufi Message* II, pp 18–19.
6 Capra, *Turning Point*, p 69.
7 Miahia Kaku and Jennifer Trainer, *The Cosmic Quest for the Theory of the Universe*.
8 *The Sufi Message* II, p 18.
9 *The Sufi Message*, XI, p 22.
10 ibid, p 9.
11 ibid, p 57.
12 ibid.
13 ibid, pp. 60–61.
14 *The Sufi Message*, II, p 18.
15 F Capra, *The Tao of Physics*, Shambala, Boulder, 1975, p 223.
16 *The Sufi Message* XI, p 69.
17 Capra, *Turning Point*, p 83.
18 ibid, p 70.
19 ibid.
20 *The Sufi Message* XI, pp. 50–51.
21 G Murchie, *Music of the Spheres*, II, Dover, New York, 1967, p 262.
22 *Art meets Science and Spirituality in a Changing Economy*, The Hague, 1990, p. 61.
23 Inayat Khan, *The Soul, Whence and Whither*, East–West Publications, London/The Hague, 1984, p 41. Elsewhere, Inayat Khan defines 'soul' as that extent of radiance or intelligence that is found particularly in the human being.
24 ibid, p 9.
25 *The Sufi Message* V, p 26.
26 Inayat Khan, *The Soul*, p 9.
27 ibid, p 15.
28 ibid, p 26.
29 ibid, pp 9–10.
30 ibid, p 15.
31 Murchie, *Music of the Spheres*, I, pp 218–19.

Chapter 6

1 Hazrat Inayat Khan, *The Soul, Whence and Whither*, East–West Publications, London/The Hague, 1984.
2 ibid, p 52 with some minor corrections based on the original texts of the lectures as published in *Complete Works of Pir-o-Murshid Hazrat Inayat Khan (original texts): Lectures on Sufism, 1923, II*, East–West Publications, London/The Hague, 1989.
3 Inayat Khan, *The Soul*, pp 23–4.
4 ibid, p 20.
5 ibid, p 21, with some corrections based on the original texts in the *Complete Works*.
6 ibid, p 29.
7 ibid, p 38.
8 ibid, p 173.
9 ibid, p 47.
10 ibid, p 48.
11 ibid, p 55.
12 ibid, p 71.
13 ibid, p 71.
14 ibid, p 74.
15 ibid, p 74.
16 L Hoyack, *De Boodschap van Inayat Khan*, Uitgeverij Ae. E Kluwer, Deventer, p 63.
17 Inayat Khan, *The Soul*, p 76.
18 ibid, p 81.
19 ibid, p 44.
20 ibid, p 104.
21 ibid, p 104.
22 ibid, p 104.
23 ibid, pp 107–108.
24 ibid, p 112.
25 *The Sufi Message of Inayat Khan*, IV, *The Mind World*.
26 *The Sufi Message of Inayat Khan*, I. *The Purpose of Life*, p 189.
27 ibid, p 26.
28 ibid, p 26.
29 Matthew 7:7 (Authorised Version).
30 *The Sufi Message of Inayat Khan*, II, *Cosmic Language*, p 248.
31 Inayat Khan, *The Soul*, p 130.

32 ibid, p 135.
33 See R A Moody, *Life after Life*, Bantam Books, New York, 1975, and also his *Reflections on Life after Life*, Bantam Books, New York, 1977.
34 Moody, *Life after Life*, p 24.
35 Inayat Khan, *The Soul*, p 141.
36 ibid, p 160.
37 ibid, p 160.
38 ibid, p 153.
39 ibid, p 145.
40 ibid, p 145.
41 ibid, p 147.
42 Moody, *Life after Life*, p 46.
43 ibid, pp 46–7.
44 Inayat Khan, *The Soul*, p 37.
45 R A Moody, *Reflections on Life after Life*, p 32.
46 Inayat Khan, *The Soul*, p 150.
47 ibid, p 160; also p 140: 'The time of the next world is quite different from the time here.' Also Moody, *Reflections*, p 101.
48 Inayat Khan, *The Soul*, p 15.
49 ibid, p 156.
50 ibid, p 159.
51 ibid, p 159.
52 ibid, p 150.
53 ibid, p 150.
54 ibid, p 164.
55 ibid, p 171.
56 ibid, p 169.
57 ibid, p 174.
58 ibid, p 178.
59 ibid, p 174.

Chapter 7

1 Inayat Khan, *The Complete Sayings*, Omega Publications, New Lebanon, 1978, p 49.
2 *The Bhagavadgita*, New American Library, 1944, chapter XI, pp 92–3.

3 ibid, p 92.
4 The *Qur'an, sura* CXII.
5 P Carus, *The Gospel of Buddha,* Open Court Publishing Company, London, 1921, pp 5, 6.
6 Deuteronomy, 10: 12, 13 and 17–20 (Authorised Version)
7 *Bhagavadgita,* pp 95–6.
8 *The Sufi Message of Inayat Khan,* I, p 70.
9 ibid, p 70.
10 *The Sufi Message,* IX, p 89.
11 ibid, p 92.
12 ibid, p 89.
13 This happens when the human being is born: some spirit is absorbed by the material form which is our body.
14 *The Sufi Message,* XI, p 64.
15 *The Sufi Message,* XI, pp 24–5.

Chapter 8

1 *The Sufi Message of Inayat Khan,* XI, p 163.
2 *The Sufi Message, Gayan Vadan Nirtan,* p 86.
3 *The Sufi Message,* V. p 245.
4 ibid, p 250.
5 The mystical meaning of sound is an important subject to which we will return in chapter 10.
6 *The Sufi Message,* XIII, p 135.
7 ibid, p 140.
8 ibid, p 142.
9 *The Sufi Message,* IV, p 155.
10 ibid, p 172.
11 ibid, p 155.
12 ibid, p 156.
13 ibid, pp 108–109.
14 ibid, p 109.
15 ibid, p 117.

Chapter 9

1 *The Sufi Message of Inayat Khan*, IV, p 126.
2 *The Sufi message*, VIII, p 99.
3 ibid, p 99.
4 *The Sufi Message*, XIII, p 204.
5 *The Sufi Message*, VIII, p 104.
6 *The Sufi Message*, III, p 255.
7 ibid, p 239.
8 ibid, p 239.
9 ibid, p 233.
10 ibid, p 234.
11 ibid, p 240.
12 ibid, p 235.
13 ibid, p 236.
14 ibid, p 255.
15 Compare with Chapter 6, above, where this matter is also dealt with.
16 *The Sufi Message*, VIII, p 104.
17 *The Sufi Message*, V, p 240.
18 *The Sufi Message*, XIII, p 175.
19 ibid, p 189.
20 Inayat Khan, *The Complete Sayings*, p 8.
21 *The Sufi Message*, XIII, p 191.
22 See Rumi's poem quoted on pp 10–12.
23 Yasna 33.14 in *The Divine Songs of Zarathustra*, edited by I J S Tareporewala, Bombay, 1951, p 348 (free English rendering).
24 *The Sufi Message*, III, p 255.

Chapter 10

1 See chapter 5 above, esp. pp 55–62.
2 *The Sufi Message of Inayat Khan*, II, pp 37–8.
3 ibid, p 14.
4 John 1:1.
5 *The Sufi Message*, VIII, pp 62–7.
6 J E Berendt, *Nada Brahma*, East–West Publications, London/ The Hague, 1988, esp. chapter IX.

7   *The Sufi Message*, II, p 124.
8   ibid, p 124.
9   ibid, p 130.
10 ibid, p 148.
11 See chapter 5, above, p 55.
12 Berendt, *Nada Brahma*, pp 46, 47.
13 G Murchie, *Music of the Spheres*, II, Dover, New York, 1967, p 338.
14 ibid, p 261.
15 ibid, p 342.
16 Murchie, *Music of the Spheres*, I, p 85. This progression, discovered by the German astronomer Johann Elert Bode, was developed into the so-called Bode's Law.
17 Berendt, *Nada Brahma*, p 104.
18 *The Sufi Message*, II, p 149.
19 ibid, p 149.
20 *The Sufi Message*, IV, p 217.
21 *The Sufi Message*, II, p 118.
22 ibid, p 119.
23 ibid, p 148.
24 See chapter 8, Mysticism: Unity with God.
25 *The Sufi Message*, II, p 151.
26 ibid, p 149.
27 ibid, n 25.
28 ibid, p 152.
29 See chapter 2, above, p 32.

Chapter 11

1   *The Sufi Message of Inayat Khan*, IV, p 15.
2   ibid, p 18.
3   ibid, p 19.
4   ibid, p 15.
5   ibid, p 20.
6   ibid, p 36.
7   ibid, p 21.
8   *The Sufi Message*, V, p 235.

9   *The Sufi Message*, IV, p 49.
10 See Deepak Chopra, *Quantum Healing, Exploring the Frontiers of Mind/Body Medicine*, New York, 1989.
11 *The Sufi Message*, IV, p 54.
12 ibid, p 55.
13 ibid, p 39.
14 See Chopra, *Quantum Healing*, p 76.
15 *The Sufi Message*, IV, p 43.
16 ibid, p 33.
17 ibid, p 24.
18 ibid, pp 25, 26.
19 See Chopra, *Quantum Healing*, p 259.
20 *The Sufi Message*, IV, p 33.
21 ibid, p 88.
22 See Chopra, *Quantum Healing*, p 73.
23 *The Sufi Message*, IV, p 32.
24 ibid, p 46.
25 ibid, pp 33, 34.
26 From the unpublished series of 'Sangatha I', p 1.
27 ibid, p 34.
28 *The Sufi Message*, pp 107, 108.
29 See Chopra, *Quantum Healing*, p 237.
30 *The Sufi Message*, IV, p 89.
31 ibid, p 76.
32 ibid, pp 80–87.
33 ibid, p 87.
34 ibid, p 85.
35 ibid, p 87.

Chapter 12

1   *The Complete Sayings of Hazrat Inayat Khan*, p 65.
2   ibid, p 202.
3   These teachings originated in America in an earlier period of Inayat Khan's teaching. They were written down by Samuel Lewis. But the deep inspiration in many passages carries the unmistakable sound of Inayat Khan's unique voice.

4 See chapter 9, p 90.

5 Walter Lippmann, *The Public Philosophy*, Chatto & Windus, London, 1955, pp 127–8.

6 Aldous Huxley, *The Perennial Philosophy*, Chatto & Windus, London, 1947, p 220.

7 Quoted by Lippman in *Public Philosophy*, p 130.

8 ibid, p 132.

9 ibid, p 127.

10 'The Book of Peace', chapter 1, p 2.

11 ibid, chapter 3, p 6.

12 'The Book of Peace', chapter 2, p 3.

13 ibid, p 4.

14 Immanuel Kant, *Toward eternal peace*, Wereld Bibliotheek, Amsterdam, 1915, in the beginning of the first appendix are 'the guarantees for eternal peace'.

15 Quoted by G. Murchie in *The Seven Mysteries of Life*, Houghton Mifflin, Boston, 1978, p 514.

16 See *WIDER Study Group Series No. 4: World Economic Summits*, Helsinki, 1989.

17 'The Book of Peace', chapter 2, p 6.

18 See *Encyclopaedia Britannica: Micropedia*, I, p 707.

19 'The Book of Peace', chapter 2, p 6.

20 ibid, p 6.

21 ibid, p 6.

22 'The Book of Peace', chapter 3, p 4.

23 ibid, p 1.

Bibliography

Hazrat Inayat Khan

The Complete Sayings of Hazrat Inayat Khan, Omega Publications, New Lebanon, 1978

The Complete Works of Pir-o-Murshid Hazrat Inayat Khan (original texts in five volumes): *Lectures on Sufism, 1923, Volume 1, January –June*, East–West Publications, London/The Hague, 1989

The Flower Garden of Inayat Khan, East–West Publications, London/The Hague, 1978.

The Soul, Whence and Whither?, East–West Publications, London/The Hague, 1984

The Sufi Message of Inayat Khan, Volumes I–XIII, Barrie and Jenkins, London/Servire Publishers, Katwijk, Holland, 1960–82. Revised edition: Volume II and Volume VIII, Element Books, Shaftesbury, 1991; Volume VI and Volume XIV, East–West Publications, London/The Hague, 1996

Books about Inayat Khan

Biography of Pir-o-Murshid Inayat Khan, East–West Publications, London/The Hague, 1979

Hoyack, L, *De Boodschep van Inayat Khan*, E Kluwer, Deventer

de Jong-Keesing, E, *Inayat Khan: a Biography*, East–West Publications, London/The Hague, 1974

—, *Inayat Answers*, East–West Publications, London/The Hague, 1977 van Stolk, S, with D Dunlop, *Memories of a Sufi Sage: Hazrat Inayat Khan*, East – West Publications, London/The Hague, 1967

Other Sufi Writings

Arberry, A J (transl.), *Mystical Poems of Rumi*, University of Chicago Press, London, 1968

The Bustan of Saadi, Wisdom of the East Series, John Murray, London, 1911

Nicholson, R A, *The Mathnawi of Jelal-ud-Din Rumi*, E J W Gibb Memorial Series, New Series, IV, 2, Lucas, London, 1972

Poems from the Divan of Hafiz, Javidan Publications, 1963

Rehatsek, E (transl.), *The Gulistan or Rose Garden of Saadi*, George Allen & Unwin, London, 1964

General

Arberry, A J, *Introduction to the History of Sufism*, Longman, Green, London, 1942

—, *Sufism: An Account of the Mysticism of Islam*, George Allen & Unwin, London, 1950

Art Meets Science and Spirituality in a Changing Economy, SDU, The Hague, 1990

Begg, W D, *The Holy Biography of Hazrat Khwaja Muin-ud-Din Chishti*, W D Begg, Ajmer, 1960

Berendt, J E, *Nada Brahma*, East–West Publications, London/The Hague, 1988

The Bhagavadgita, New American Library, New York/Scarborough, Ontario, 1944

Capra, F, *The Turning Point*, Wildwood House, London, 1982

—, *The Tao of Physics*, Shambala, Boulder, 1975

Carus, P, *The Gospel of Buddha*, Open Court Publishing, London 1921

Chopra, Deepak, *Quantum Healing: Exploring the Frontiers of Mind/Body Medicine*, Bantam Books, New York, 1989

The Divine Songs of Zarathrustra, I J S Taraporewala (ed.), D B Taraporewala Sons and Company, Bombay, 1951

Hoyack, L, 'De Wijsheid van Hermes Trismegistus', in *De Soefie Gedachte*, September 1954

Huxley, A, *The Perennial Philosophy*, Chatto & Windus, London, 1947

Kaku, M, and J Trainer, *The Cosmic Quest for the Theory of the Universe*

Khan, Murshid Musharaff, *Pages in the Life of a Sufi* (third edition), East–West Publications, London/The Hague, 1982

Kant, I, *Toward Eternal Peace*, Wereld Bibliotheek, Amsterdam, 1915

The Kybalion, Yogi Publication Society, Chicago, 1908

Lippmann, W, *The Public Philosophy*, Chatto & Windus, London, 1955

Moody, R A, *Life After Life*, Bantam Books, New York, 1975

—, *Reflections on Life After Life*, Bantam Books, New York, 1977

Murchie, G, *Music of the Spheres*, I and II, Dover Publications, New York, 1967

—, *The Seven Mysteries of Life*, Houghton Mifflin, Boston, 1978

Nawn, Munira, [writing in] *Forty Years of Sufism (Sufi Quarterly Special Issue)*, 1950

Sharib, Zahurul Hassan, *Khwaja Gharib Nawaz*, S H Muhammad Ashraf, Lahare, 1961

WIDER Study Group Series 4: World Economic Summits, Helsinki, 1989

Useful Addresses

Requests for information about the International Sufi Movement founded by Hazrat Inayat Khan to be sent to:

The General Secretariat of the Sufi Movement
Anna Paulownastraat 78
2518 BJ The Hague
The Netherlands
Telephone: 31 (0)70 346 1594
Fax: 31 (0)70 361 4864

Internet address of Sufi Center Bookstore:
        http://guess.worldweb.net/sufi
E-mail address: jmccaig@worldweb.net

Index